THIS IS
DOWN WIND
SAILING

THIS IS
DOWN WIND
SAILING

John Oakeley

Copyright © United Nautical Publishers SA
Basel, Switzerland 1981

First published in the United States 1981 by
SAIL BOOKS division of Sail Publications Inc,
34 Commercial Wharf,
Boston Massachusetts 02110

ISBN 0–914814–29–X

Distributed to bookstores by
W. W. Norton & Co. Inc.

Printed in Italy by Grafiche Editoriali Padane, Cremona

Picture credits

Daniel Forster
Pages 9, 36, 39, 50, 89, 108

Malcolm Donald
Pages 44, 61, 75, 110

Alastair Black
Pages 63, 126, 127

Brian Manby
Pages 24, 94

Remaining photographs by
Richard Creagh-Osborne and John Oakeley

Drawing and diagrams

Peter Milne

Contents

Introduction

Down wind sailing can be easy, relaxing and the very opposite to the hard, wet slog of a boat smashing its way to windward. After all, the wind just blows your boat along in the same direction as it is going and you have nothing to do but steer – or have you?

Of course, under reduced sail, down wind sailing is indeed a quiet time. But more and more, even the family sailors want to improve the performance of their boats, not only to make sea passages faster or more reliably, but because a boat which is leaping forward down the face of the waves under a heavy press of multicoloured straining sailcloth is just the most exciting thing afloat. In these conditions the whole crew is at a peak of excitement and tension in its efforts to control the power of the wind on the rig, and the waves on the hull, and to hold the boat steady and level so as to gain every scrap of available speed.

For a boat to surf at 15 knots is not unusual, but it needs a slick, well-trained crew to keep it up and, even more, to carry out manoeuvres such as gybing, peel-changes or big-boy setting in tough conditions.

The cruising owner, of course, has plenty of time. He can run off to leeward when preparing to gybe, for example, which would be unacceptable to the racing crew. Similarly he would use safe and sure techniques with his smaller and less experienced crew, even to lowering spinnaker, gybing, and re-hoisting if he felt it prudent. However there is no doubt that the developments that are continually taking place on the racing circuits bring benefits a year or two later to cruising owners in better gear, better and often simpler techniques and improved cuts of sail. The so-called 'cruising chutes' which set without a pole are an example of making life easy for the weekend down wind sailor.

I offer no apology therefore for concentrating on racing gear and its handling in this book, for what is a one-off racing 'special' today is frequently a universal technique next year. Besides, the racing crews have not only learnt how to set and trim sails to perfection, which improves speed, but also have altered, adjusted and refined the shapes of sails and the details of gear so that the whole operation of handling and manoeuvring the boat is safer. After all, a racing crew does not want to lose control in a race since this wastes valuable time. Thus ever more powerful rigs are carried in ever more tough conditions with the same crew strength. De-tuned for cruising purposes this is translated into safer but faster passage making and simpler, more foolproof gear and techniques.

Apart from the actual gear and sails, and the best ways of setting, handling and lowering them in many different conditions, I have also touched on the basic tactical manoeuvres of down wind racing and the best sailing angles for different down wind sails. Many owners want to race at some time, even if it is only a weekend cruiser race to a nearby port and so some simple information on how to get the best out of a boat and crew could be useful to them. Planning a passage across open water in the best way also may involve setting the right combination of sails for a downhill ride with a change of course at some point to keep up the speed when forecast weather conditions change. Knowing the likely performance of the boat, and possible handling problems of the rig, could be worth while.

I hope that a study of this handbook will make sailing and racing more interesting, safer, and more fun for everyone.

John D. A. Oakeley
Warsash, 1980

Equipment required

Key:
1 Spinnaker boom
2 Spinnaker boom cup and slider
3 Spinnaker boom deck stowage point
4 Spinnaker
5 Jockey pole
6 Sheave in jockey pole end
7 Spinnaker guy and lazy sheet
8 Spinnaker sheet and lazy guy
9 Snap shackle attachment for spinnaker guy
10 Snap shackle attachment for spinnaker sheet
11 Twin turning blocks; the after sheave for the spinnaker sheet, the forward sheave for the big-boy or light sheet
12 Turning block for spinnaker guy
13 Stopper for spinnaker guy
14 Guide sheave for spinnaker sheet
15 Stopper for spinnaker sheet
16 Winches for guy
17 Winches for sheet
18 Winches for spinnaker boom lift
19 Winch for spinnaker boom downhaul
20 Big-boy or light spinnaker sheet
21 Snap shackle for light sheet
22 Spinnaker boom foreguy
23 Track and slider for spinnaker staysail or tall-boy
24 Turning block for spinnaker foreguy
25 Heel lift rope
26 Heel downhaul
27 Cleat for the heel lift uphaul and downhaul
28 Spinnaker boom track with slider
29 Spinnaker boom lift
30 Spinnaker halyard
31 Spinnaker halyard block
32 Spinnaker boom end
33 Spinnaker boom release toggle
34 Peeling strop (5 feet long)

A

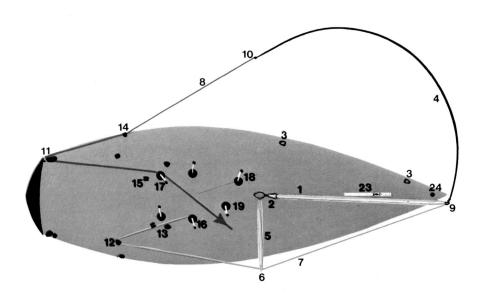

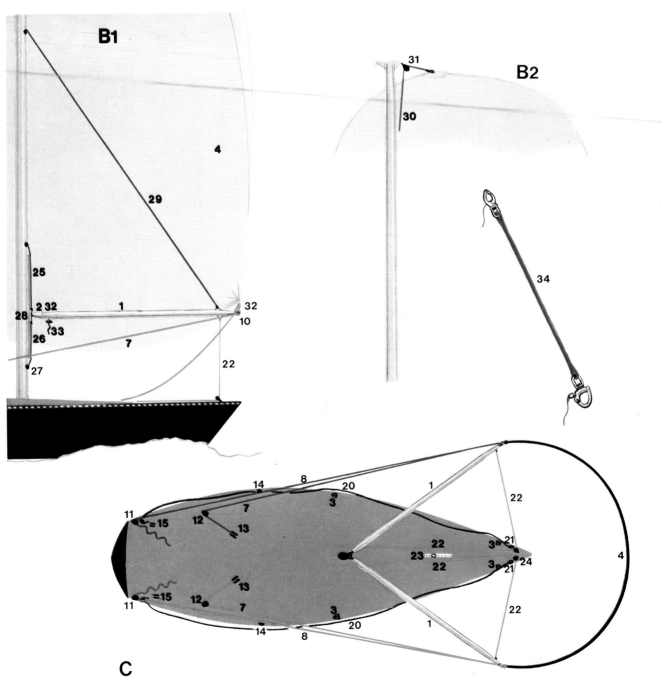

B1

4

29

25

2 32
28
33
26
27

1

7

32
10

22

B2

31

30

34

11

14
8
20
1
22

11
=15
12
7
13
3

22
23
3
21
24
22
3
21

12
13

11
=15
12
7
14
8
20
3
1
22

4

C

Masthead fittings

Spinnaker halyard attachments at the masthead vary a great deal; here are four types arranged to take the normal twin halyards.

A is the most common and is standard on most cruising boats. Each arm carries a spinnaker halyard block on a swivel. The halyard can then either pass down the fore side of the mast externally, or it can enter a slot on the front of the mast a little below the mainsail measurement band and exit about 6 feet above deck level.

The next three illustrations are variations on a theme.

B has a pair of swivelling blocks which are inset into the mast section. The halyards go over these blocks and then pass internally down the mast. The advantage of this system is that it reduces the amount of windage and, since the blocks can swivel through 90°, friction is reduced to the minimum.

C has the spinnaker halyards entering the mast through two bull's eyes which are made either of stainless steel or ceramic. After entering the bull's eyes the halyards then go over two sheaves and pass internally down the mast. This arrangement

reduces windage and weight, but the bull's eyes will cause more friction when hoisting on a shy reach.

D has two sets of built-in sheaves, the lower ones for the genoa halyards, the upper pair for the spinnaker halyards. The spinnaker halyard sheaves are lined either side with stainless steel, and the forestay attachment is built up and rounded for the first 8 inches or so to give a reasonable bearing surface when the windward spinnaker halyard passes over the top. This design probably has the lowest windage and also the lightest mast-

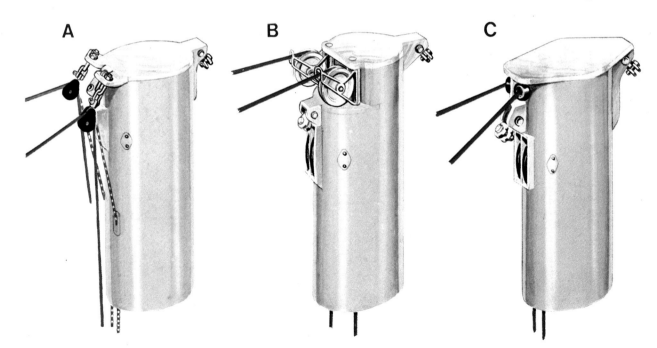

A   B   C

head; the upper sheaves are also used for genoas and bloopers.

For racing use I believe that **B** and **D** are the best methods, while the long-distance cruising boat should have **A** with external halyards, the advantage here being that it is then possible to end-for-end the halyards without unreeving them, since the blocks have swivels. Also, should the halyard break it is very easy to reeve another.

D

Spinnaker booms

There are many and varied types. Here I have illustrated just two.

A is a typical boom as used on ocean racers and serious 'round-the-cans' campaigners. This type has a hook outer end with a rotating plunger type of locking pin. This can be operated from the outboard end (**a**), or it can have internal attachments which emerge through a small sheave cage on the underside of the inboard end, with a toggle on the end of the tripping line (**b**).

There are two types of outboard end. The first is illustrated on drawing **B** at **f**. On the second type, **c** on drawing **A**, having pulled the pin open, it is locked in that position by the trigger at **d**. This is a big advantage when gybing quickly since all you have to do is bang the new guy into the spinnaker boom end. The guy touches the trigger at **d** and lets off the plunger. Be careful not to have your finger in the way!

The inboard end of type **A** fits into a cup and is located there by a

spring-loaded plunger on the underside (**e**). This type of spinnaker boom is ideal for single-pole dip gybing, or for the twin-pole method. A point to note is that the inboard end release system is seldom made long enough. Manufacturers forget that the normal gybing position on a big boat means that the boom is a long way above the deck. You normally have to tie a sail tie or lanyard to the toggle to make it long enough for the crew to be able to reach it (**g**).

B shows a spinnaker boom that can be used on the smaller yachts. Notice that both ends are identical (**f**) and this makes it ideal for end-for-end gybing. The inboard end can be attached to the normal fixed eye on the front of the mast (**h**) or to a stirrup and slide (**j**). This stirrup is superior to the eye as it has a much better swivelling movement. With an eye there is a great deal of friction when swinging the boom fore and aft, as the hook end has to slide round the ring.

The spinnaker boom ends (**f**) are opened by banging them on the ring on the mast so that the angled lead-in opens the plunger to allow it to snap on. When fitting trip lines to a double ended boom it is essential that they are not joined together since, when you want to release one end or the other, you apply pressure on to the line and it is more than likely that you will open both ends at once. Each trip line should be fastened to its own little eyelet at the opposite end (**k**) but make sure that this is sufficiently far off centre to enable the operator to grab the line quickly without getting hold of both of them. The spinnaker lift on this type of boom should always be taken from the centre point (**1**) as this helps to balance the boom when gybing. The downhaul should, whenever possible, also be taken from the centre but, because of the extra pressure, it should be spread by a bridle fixed to the ends.

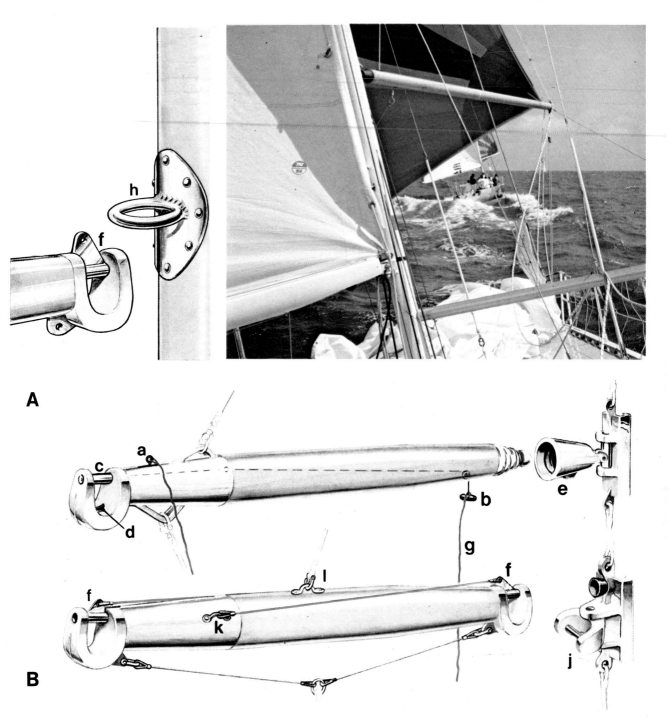

A

B

Reaching strut

When reaching the spinnaker guys are often led down to snatch blocks which are fastened to the toe rail at the base of the shrouds. This is a method of keeping the spinnaker guy away from the shrouds and gives a better angle to the lead of the guy. Be careful that the snatch block is of adequate size and that there is something solid to fasten it to.

One problem is that the same size toe rail is often fitted to any boat below 45 feet in length. The standard toe rail is strong enough to withstand the strains imposed by the guy on boats of half a ton and below, but is border-line at the three-quarter ton rating, and is certainly not adequate above. It always worries me when I see the spinnaker trimmer standing up by the shrouds so that he can get a good view of the spinnaker. One day the snatch block will break and the guy will cut his legs off just above the ankle!

This is why I prefer to use a reaching strut, also called a jockey pole. It has two advantages over the previous method; first, it holds the spinnaker guy further outboard and therefore gives a better lead, and second, the spinnaker guy is not pulled down, which would put excessive strain on the spinnaker boom lift, and this makes it easy to adjust the height of the outboard end.

Reaching struts should always have a sheave in the outboard end with a projecting tongue on the lower side (**m**) so that when the guy goes slack, which it can do in light weather, it does not drop off. At one-third of its distance from the outboard end there should be a strong eye on the upper side to which a lanyard can be spliced (**n**) so that the strut can be lashed to the main shrouds. This holds it level and also stops it dropping overboard should it become detached from the mast.

At the inboard end there can be a fitting rather similar to those on spinnaker booms which attach to a fixed eye on the side of the mast. The disadvantage of this is that a fixed eye is more likely to catch sheets when tacking. I favour a spigot end which fits into a reinforced hole on the side of the mast (**p**), since the strain on the reaching strut is pure compression and the pole itself is fastened to the shrouds by a lanyard. It very seldom comes out and there is no obstruction for halyards or sheets to catch.

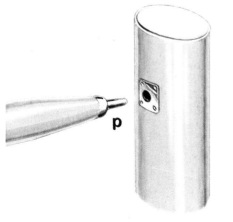

Mast attachments

A shows the commonest way of attaching the pole to the mast which consists of a rather heavy eye on a large base plate. It is screwed or riveted to the mast at the position which sets the pole at about the correct height in medium wind strengths. If your boat is fitted with this type of attachment, and you want to race, it is essential to have a duplicate ring placed some way below it so that, when the wind is lighter, the whole spinnaker pole can be moved downwards. There is a snag to having this type of ring, especially when fitted low down – the sheets, when passing across the front of the mast during a tack, are very likely to catch on it.

B shows the same heavy duty eye welded to a slide which is fitted to a track on the front of the mast. This is a great improvement over the fixed eye since it can be adjusted in height. When not in use it can also be pushed right up to the top of the track or right down to the bottom to get it out of the way of the sheets. Normally there is a spring-loaded plunger-type locating pin which fits into a hole drilled in the track, so that you can lock the eye in any given position.

C shows a cup and slider which is more commonly found in boats over 30 feet in length. This cup fitting marries with the pole end and is used because it forms a better 'goose-neck' or universal joint. The

end of the spinnaker pole fits inside the bell and a little catch locates the latter in a groove on the spinnaker boom end fitting, thus locking it in place.

D shows an even more advanced design which consists of a saddle that fits around the fore side of the mast. It has PTFE bearing points (low-friction poly-tetra-fluor-ethylene) fitted on the inside surface. The eye or cup can be fastened to the forward side. The advantage of this type of fitting is that it reduces the amount of windage to the barest minimum, since it does not use a projecting track on the forward side of the mast, while still being adjustable for height.

To position these various attachments one can use the spring-loaded

plunger but if, as in larger boats, the spinnaker boom attachment point, a its uppermost limit of travel, is above the reach of a man one has to use a spinnaker boom heel lift and down haul as shown in figures **E** and **F**.

E shows a suitable method for use on a large yacht, which has a winch to control the forces, but the external lift and downhaul, though easy to fit and maintain, has appreciable wind resistance.

F is an internal system, without a winch, which can be used on smaller boats and has low windage. You can even operate this system from the cockpit by making the lower part of the control line much longer and taking it through two turning blocks at the base of the mast and back through a small winch-cum-cleat or the cockpit coaming. Then the spinnaker pole heel can be moved without you going forward, which can be a big advantage on boats of 30 feet and below when it is blowing hard since the crew's weight in the bow would slow her down.

Remember, when moving the inboard end of the spinnaker pole up or down, that there is a great deal of pressure on the slide, so you should never get the pole at too great an angle to the horizontal. The compression can force the heel of the pole downwards and along the track so that it can even break the endstop. It takes a lot of effort to prevent this movement and it will be nearly impossible to lift the inboard end again. When heavily loaded, try moving it only 12 to 18 inches first and then lower or lift the outboard end, so restoring the spinnaker boom to level, before shifting it any more.

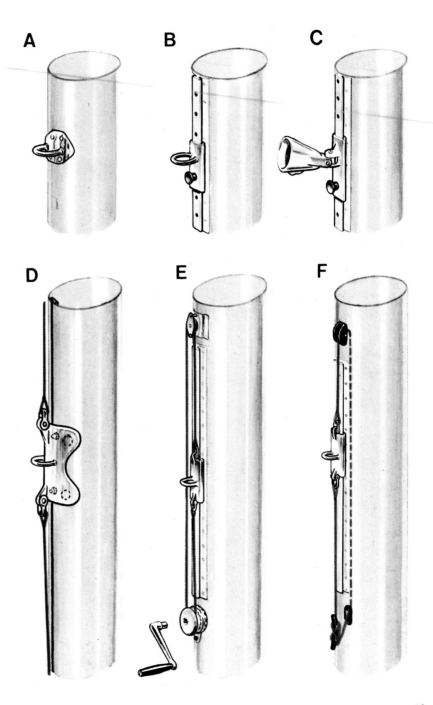

Halyards, sheets and snap shackles

The universal method for attaching halyards and sheets to spinnakers and guys to sheets is with snap shackles, but they differ in design details according to where they are to be used.

A shows a halyard snap shackle which includes a swivel. It is not necessary to fit a swivel snap shackle on the spinnaker halyard when there is already a swivel on the head of the sail, but the halyard may also double for the genoa and the swivel prevents the wire from getting twists into it.

B shows the best type of snap shackle for the spinnaker sheet. It is top hinged which allows it to be opened when under load. This is very important particularly when releasing the tack of the spinnaker from the end of the pole when on a shy reach. This shackle is made in California and has no lanyard, and will not open accidentally.

More ordinary snap shackles with side action are usually sold without any type of lanyard for pulling the pin. The ring or knob supplied is usually too small to grip. You should add your own lanyards before you start using them. **a**, **b** and **c** are three fitted lanyards, but the only correct one is type **a** which is a straight plaited cord about 2½ inches long, heat sealed or whipped at the outboard end.

The other two methods are not recommended. Type **b**, with a knot in the end, and type **c**, with a loop, can catch and open the shackle when not wanted. For example, when you are hoisting the spinnaker, the lanyard could hook over the hanks on the genoa, thereby tripping the snap shackle and releasing the spinnaker. Type **a**, on the other hand, has very little friction until it is gripped. The shackle on the guy can be taped up as an extra precaution. Unfortunately side-action shackles will sooner or later open if the sail flogs.

On many racing boats you can see the foredeck crew having great difficulty in getting the guy out of the spinnaker boom end when trying to gybe. This hang-up is often caused by the tapered splice in the end of the guy being pulled tight into the spinnaker boom end so that, when the spinnaker boom plunger is tripped, the guy is found to be wedged in. A simple way to avoid this is to fit a 2½×2½ inch disc, made of nylon or reinforced plastic, over the spinnaker guy and slide it up until it rests on the splice, as in **C**. The disc then lies against the spinnaker boom end and makes gybing very much easier.

Wire and rope sizes

The table on the right shows the recommended sizes for wires and ropes for spinnaker and headsail handling.

The wire diameters are based on 7×19 construction using 180 kg/mm^2 tensile strength steel. Rope diameters are based on Bridon Fibers Super Braidline or Marlow Rope 16-plait ropes or others of equivalent breaking strength.

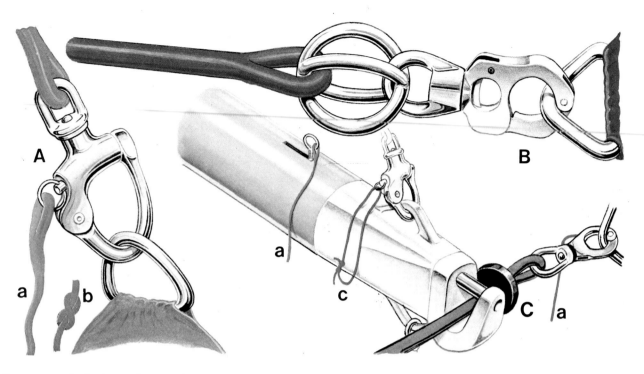

Recommended wire and rope sizes

Item	Mini-tonner		¼ tonner		½ tonner		¾ tonner		1 tonner		2 tonner		3 tonner	
	Wire	*Rope*	*Wire*	*Rope*	*Wire*	*Rope*	*Wire*	*Rope*	*Wire*	*Rope*	*Wire*	*Rope*	*Wire*	*Rope*
Genoa halyard	4	8	4	8	5	10	5	10	5	10	6	10	7	12
Spinnaker halyard	3	8	4	8	4	10	5	10	5	10	6	10	6	12
Main halyard	3	8	4	8	4	10	4	10	5	10	5	10	6	12
Standing main boom topping lift	2		2		2		2		2.5		3		4	
Spinnaker boom topping lift	2.5	7	3	7	4	8	4	8	4	10	5	10	5	
Genoa sheets		10		10		10		12		14		16		18
Mainsheet		8		8		8		10		10		12		12
Spinnaker guy		10		10		10		12		14		16		18
Spinnaker sheet		8		8		8		10		10		12		12
Spinnaker foreguy		8		8		8		10		10		12		14
Light spinnaker sheet		3		3		3		4		5		6		8
Big-boy sheet		6		7		7		8		8		10		12
Slab reef lines		7		7		8		8		8		10		12
Light genoa sheets		4		4		4		5		6		7		8

Cleats and stoppers

The introduction of purpose designed halyard and sheet jammers and stoppers makes it very much easier to handle a yacht. It also cuts down the number of winches to the extent that you can have as many as three ropes going to one winch. When laying out a system of operation, the ropes leading to one winch must be such that they do not have to be handled at the same time. They can then be led through jammers or stoppers before going to a winch. When the sheet or halyard has been tensioned it can be jammed off, leaving the winch available for operating one of the other lines (*opposite*).

The jammer should always act on rope, not wire. Wire halyards and sheets should have rope tails with the splice positioned on the mast side of the jammer when fully taut.

One of the cheapest jamming cleats on the market is the clam-cleat (**B**). Provided it is positioned exactly underneath the rope when under tension, it is a simple matter to push the rope down into this type of jammer as you ease off on the winch.

However unjamming a clam-cleat is not so easy when there is a heavy tension on the rope. But there is a type which has a hinged base plate and a removable pin at the after end; the cleat then tips up and releases the rope. So this simple device can now also be used as a rope stopper for quite heavily loaded lines.

The lever-cam jammers which are arranged vertically (*bottom left*) are ideal for halyards, especially those that lead from turning blocks at the base of the mast and then to a winch.

Horizontally fitted lever-cam jammers are ideal for spinnaker sheets, spinnaker guys or genoa sheets (*bottom right*). For example, when gybing the spinnaker with double poles, it is possible to jam off the guy and sheet at the moment of gybing, thus freeing the winches, and then you can put the new guy and the new sheet on to the same winches.

The success of all types of jamming cleats used as stoppers relies on their being placed exactly in line with the turning point of the rope and the winch itself.

Standard cleats are used to back up temporary jammers or winches. They should have wide bases for adequate security, and be set so that the horns are at any angle of about 30° to the lead of the rope (**A**).

A

B

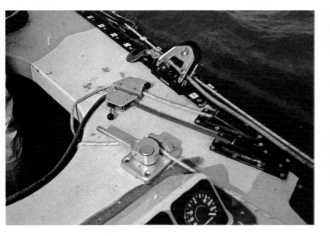

Winches and turning blocks

Winches

Winches are very expensive and so their use and position has to be pre-considered. For example:

Only fit winches where you are absolutely certain you need them.

Make one winch do a number of jobs with the aid of carefully sited stoppers and jammers.

When positioning a winch make sure that the handle can swing clear of obstructions for its full circle. Many winches are fitted too close to lifelines. After a three-quarter turn of the handle you then take the skin off your knuckles.

Winches are powerful machines and therefore have to be very securely fastened to the boat. Follow the manufacturer's instructions exactly. Handles can have short cranks, long cranks, ratchet action, and single or double grips. The most powerful is the double grip type; in emergency two people can wind. The ratchet handle is excellent if you need to put a lot of force into a small amount of movement. It is ideal for runner winches.

A handle should never be left in the winch. It could do serious damage to

someone falling on it. Therefore each handle must have its own holder where the winch operator can easily reach it. Site the holder so that the bights of rope cannot catch round the handle and pull it out.

Self-tailing or standard winches? Self-tailers (*top right*) are ideal for one-man operations such as spinnaker boom hoist, spinnaker guy, foreguy, or runner winches, but are not necessary for winches that need two men, such as genoa and spinnaker sheet winches.

The table gives some recommended winch sizes as a guide both for racing and cruising uses.

Turning blocks

Down wind sails normally need only blocks which can be shackled to various positions on the toe rails or deck tracks. The main turning blocks for the genoa sheets, which are on tracks bolted securely to the decks, are seldom needed for spinnaker sheets and guys. There are many different designs but the best are very strongly constructed and will have roller bearings for the sheaves.

Recommended winch sizes

	LOA (feet)	20 to 25	25 to 27	30 to 32	33 to 35	35 to 36	36 to 39	40 to 41	42 to 43	44 to 48	50 to 55	60+
	LOA (metres)	6.0 to 7.6	7.6 to 8.25	9.1 to 9.75	10.0 to 10.7	10.7 to 11.0	11.0 to 12.0	12 to 12.50	12.80 to 13.0	13.40 to 14.60	15.30 to 16.80	18.30+
Lewmar	Class	Mini-tonner	¼ tonner	½ tonner	¾ tonner	1 tonner	1 tonner	2 tonner	2 tonner			
Sail areas in square feet and square metres	Genoa	200/19	300/28	350/33	470/44	550/51	600/56	750/70	900/84	1100/102	1500/140	2000/186
	Spinnaker	300/28	400/37	600/56	800/74	1000/93	1200/111	1400/130	1600/149	1900/177	3000/279	4000/372
	Main	120/11	150/14	180/17	210/20	230/21	260/24	300/28	350/33	420/39	750/70	1200/111
Genoa sheet	Racing	8	16 or 30	30 or 40	43 or 44	44 or 48	48 or 55	55	55 or 65	65 or 80	95 or 96	95 or 96
	Cruising	7	10 or 16	30	40	43 or 44	44	44 or 48	48 or 55	55 or 65	65 or 80	80 or 95
Spinnaker sheet	Racing	6	8	10 or 16	30 or 40	40 or 43	43	44	44 or 48	48 or 55	55 or 65	65
	Cruising	6	7	8 or 10	16 or 30	30	30 or 40	40	44	48	55	55
Main-sheet	Racing		6	8	16	30	30	40	40	43 or 55	44	48
	Cruising		6	6	7 or 10	10 or 16	16	30	30	40	43	44
Genoa halyard	Racing	8	16	30	30 or 40	40 or 43	44	44	44 or 48	48 or 55	55 or 65	65
	Cruising	6	7	8 or 16	16 or 30	30	40 or 43	43	44	44	48	48 or 55
Spinnaker halyard	Racing	6	8	16	30	40	40 or 43	43	43	44 or 48	48 or 55	55
	Cruising	6	7	7	8 or 10	16	16 or 30	30	40	43	44	48
Main halyard	Racing	6	6	8	10 or 16	30 or 40	40 or 1H	40 or 2H	40 or 2.2H	44 or 3H	44 or 3H	48 or 3H
	Cruising	6	6	7	8 or 10	16 or 1H	16 or 1H	30 or 2H	30 or 2H	40 or 2.2H	43 or 2.2H	44 or 3H
Staysail halyard	Racing	8	8	16	30	30 or 40	40	40 or 43	43	44	48	55
	Cruising	6	6 or 7	8	8 or 10	10 or 16	16	16 or 30	30 or 40	40	44	44 or 48
Spin pole topping lift	Racing				7 or 8	8 or 10	10	10 or 16	16 or 30	30	40	43
	Cruising				6	8	8 or 10	10	16	16	30	40
Spin pole foreguy	Racing		6	6	8	10 or 16	16	16 or 30	30	40	43	44
	Cruising		6	6	7	8 or 10	8 or 10	10	16	30	40	43
Mainsail outhaul	Racing	6	6	6	6	8	8	8	8	8	16	16
	Cruising	6	6	6	6	6 or 7	7	8	8	8	8	16
Cunningham or reef	Racing	6	6	6	8	16	16 or 30	30	30 or 40	40 or 43	43 or 44	44 or 48
	Cruising	6	6	6	6 or 7	7	8	16	30	30	40	43
Boom vang	Racing	6	6	6	7 or 8	8 or 10	10	16	30	40	43	43
	Cruising	8	6	6	7	8	8	10	16	30	40	40

Spinnaker designs

Spinnaker shapes and designs are continually being developed, sometimes changing dramatically. The modern racing spinnaker, which is always symmetrical, started with the 'cross-cut' shape (**A**) often made in two halves, with a centre seam. Smaller sails had full-width panels. The main disadvantage of this cut was that the strain on the shoulders was diagonal, which allowed the cloth to stretch there, whereas the tapes did not. The result was a very hooked leech and luff at the top.

A modification was the 'radial head' (**B**) which had radiating panels in the top third which were tapered from the head to between a quarter and half height. This virtually eliminated the bias stretch so that the radial head thus flattened the leech and luff. This enabled the correct slot to be maintained between spinnaker and mainsail when reaching and the wind flowing easily round the shallow head also helped to eliminate the previously excessive heeling which made steering difficult and created leeway. This cut is still used today with great success.

The 'radial head' cut was at its best reaching when it blew hard but like other designs became very full in the lower part, so it was decided to try 'radial heads' in each corner. This worked very successfully, making the lower half much flatter and far more stable. This new 'tri-radial' cut (**C**) also made the sail

very much stronger so that lighter weight cloth could be used. In fact the 'tri-radial' became so popular that it was used on almost every occasion. But up to 10 knots of wind the radial head was still superior to the tri-radial, though over this wind speed the situation was reversed. This seemed to be because the tri-radial had too many seams in the bottom half which weighed the sail down.

The tri-radial was fine for reaching in very light conditions but a variation to save some of the seam weight was to put cross-cut seams in the clews. This seam was shaped so that it flattened the corners of the sail and so increased its reaching performance while not affecting its running ability (**E**). But such special sails are seldom seen.

The cross cut was pioneered by the British sailmaker, M & W, as was the 'jumbo foot' spinnaker (**F**). This was extra area which could be added to spinnakers of types **B**, **C** and **E**. Unlike Olympic classes the IOR has no centre seam measurement for the spinnaker; only the luffs and widths are measured. So everything you gain on the centre line is a bonus. Under tests, in 20 knots of wind, it showed a marked increase in power over a standard spinnaker. It was difficult to understand just why the increase was so large until, a year later, I discovered that it was also creating an 'end-plate' effect by stopping the

wind coming off the bottom and making it go out round the edges. Boats that had the 'jumbo foot' running spinnaker found that they could run as fast as other boats could reach but a problem was that you could not see where you were going since the droop on a two-tonner, for example, could be up to 9 feet. Another snag was running at night when the skirt could drop over the sidelights; cured by putting the sidelights inside the bow just below the deck.

Finally, the most famous type of spinnaker of all time, the Bruce Banks 'star-cut' (**D**) which was a complete breakthrough in spinnaker design. It was intended solely for very close reaching and it could be set with the spinnaker boom end about 4 feet above the stem head and sheeted down to the gunwale a little forward of the stern. The cut allowed the sail to remain very flat and stable and so it could be used almost like a genoa. This type of spinnaker can be set with the wind as close as 45° off the bow.

The 'star-cut' also had a second use because it was very flat, small and strong – it turned out to be ideal for heavy weather running. By taking a sheet through a snatch block positioned near the shrouds, and having the spinnaker boom end somewhat lower than usual, the sail became very stable and was ideally suited for this sort of sailing.

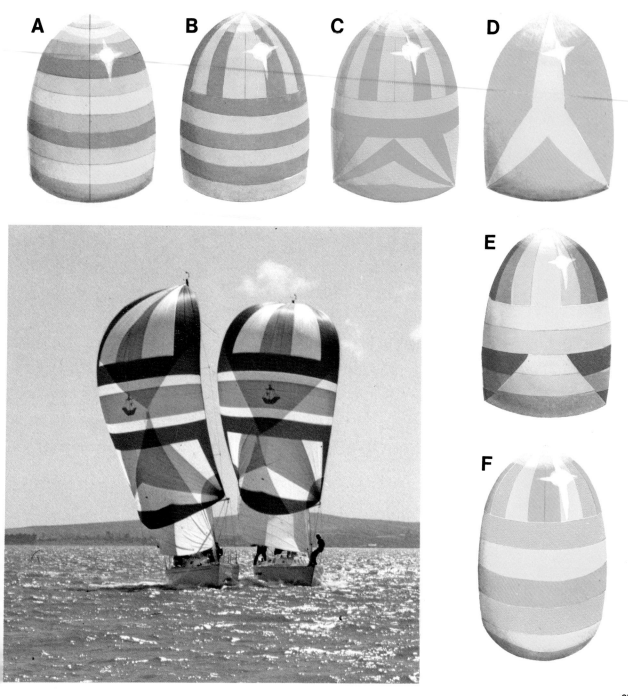

Big-boys and bloopers

Whatever they are called in different sailing areas, they are not particularly new. The first of this type that I saw was in the fifties on a boat called *Golden Vanity* on the east coast. However, since those early days the method of manufacture and the setting of these sails has improved dramatically.

There are a number of possible constructions, some of which are shown in the diagrams. The photograph shows yet another cut.

A is similar to a spinnaker with a radial head and cross-cut panels below; **B** is another similar sail but has vertical panels in the foot; **C** is similar to a standard mitred head-sail; **D** is one I have been associated with – a design with seams radiating from the centre of the luff.

Why so many different designs? I believe it to be a sail which does not behave like a spinnaker, nor is it a true headsail. Because of this it needs a new approach and type **D** is somewhere close to being the ideal design. The main problem with this sail is that the wind normally crosses from clew to luff (the concave edge) which is contrary to all other sails. The cloth has to be laid so that it can stretch easily on the foot and the leech (the convex edges). In type **D** this stretch can happen because the weakest direction of the cloth (the bias) is along these edges which allows the foot and leech to belly out to leeward.

From the back the leech and foot look just like the trailing edge of a hang-glider's wing. It produces a very stable sail which is easily set and has great pulling power.

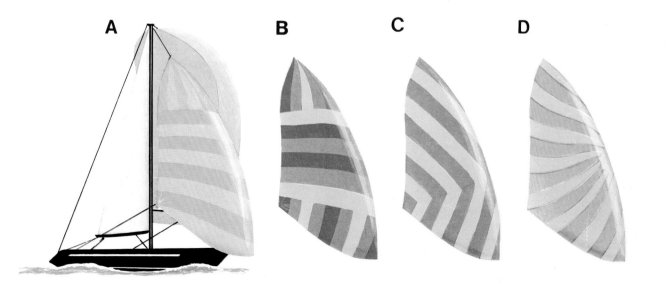

A   B   C   D

The tall-boy

The tall-boy (or slotsail as it is often called) is the type of spinnaker staysail. The conventional staysail is like an ordinary jib and merely increases free area between the mast and the spinnaker.

Slotsails are very tall and narrow and so they do not effectively reduce the amount of wind which is reaching the spinnaker. They can, if trimmed correctly (and this is often difficult to achieve) create a slot effect in combination with the mainsail, as is indicated in the diagrams opposite, so making the mainsail far more effective, especially in the lighter wind ranges.

When the wind is abeam, or further forward, the tack of the tall-boy will be positioned on the centre line (**A**). As the wind draws aft the tack can be moved out towards the windward side to improve its wind catching ability (**B**).

On rare occasions the tall-boy has been known to give an increase in speed when it is set in between the spinnaker and the big-boy on a dead run in winds over 15 knots. There is no doubt it is a difficult sail to trim,

but it can produce dramatic results in situations when the crew is having a problem in maintaining airflow over the lee side of the mainsail. Think, for example, of frustratingly light winds coupled with a slop which shakes the air out of the sails. Here, a slotsail could just provide that extra acceleration to the airflow to get the mainsail working properly. The resulting increase in drive could be well worth while.

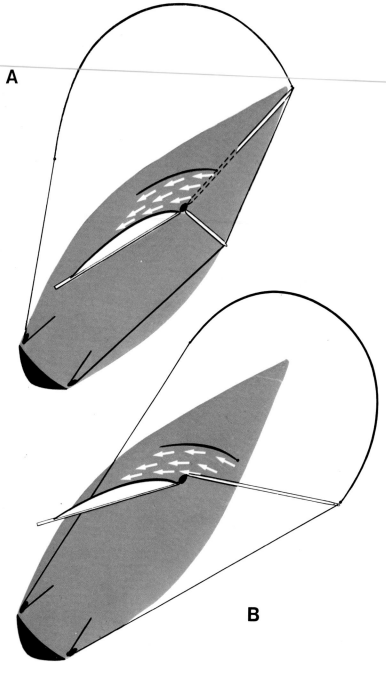

Packing equipment

Turtles, buckets and zip bags

Success or failure in setting a spinnaker depends greatly on the amount of preparation. There are three main types of spinnaker containers for the racing boat.

A shows a bucket-shaped bag, or turtle, with semi-hard rim and a lid. The lid can be a piece of canvas, with shock cord round the edge, which can be clipped over the container rim to keep the spinnaker inside and dry. This type can be used for setting from a pulpit, or from the lee shrouds.

B is a variation on this and has a top which has three segmented flaps, each of which is edged with velcro strip. There are cut-outs to allow the clews and head of the spinnaker to project once it is sealed up and, like the containers in figure **A**, it has attachment points just below the half-height to which lanyards with quick release hooks can be fastened. It is essential that all these containers are lashed down when hoisting the spinnaker or they will disappear overboard.

C shows a spinnaker sausage bag. When a spinnaker is packed into one of these, the head and clews project through the openings, and the tags can be passed through the sail cringles and fastened together (**D**). Keep the corners correctly positioned ready for attaching the halyard sheet and guy quickly.

There is velcro strip on the edges between the ties and, when closed, this keeps out most of the water. This bag should not be too large in diameter otherwise, when it is hauled out of the hatchway, the spinnaker will drop down to one end. There are ties on the bottom of the bag for attaching to the toe-rail. A sausage bag is used when setting the spinnaker to leeward of the genoa.

How to pack

To pack a spinnaker with speed really needs two people. First find the head of the sail, then each man takes one leech and coils up the tape on his edge of the sail (most spinnakers have a green and a red tape to make this job easier). When the tape is coiled up to the clew, keep a tight hold on the coil and

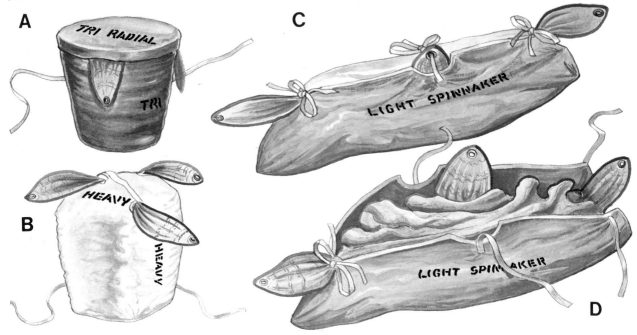

pack the loose part of the spinnaker foot first into the bag with the coil of coloured tape placed on the top and with the clews coming out on either side. The head is the last part to go into the bag. Make sure that the green side of the head patch is pointing towards the green clew and this will ensure that there is no twist in the sail. The method described is an ideal way of packing any size of floater or small spinnaker, say on yachts up to 30 feet in length.

Stopping a spinnaker

On larger boats one of the best methods of controlling a spinnaker during the hoist is by stopping it. This is done by stretching the spinnaker out, placing the red and green tapes together, then rolling up the surplus into a sausage parallel to the tapes. It is then stopped with cotton ties or very thin large diameter elastic bands. When this had been completed the spinnaker should look as it does in figure **E**. Although this system is very effec-

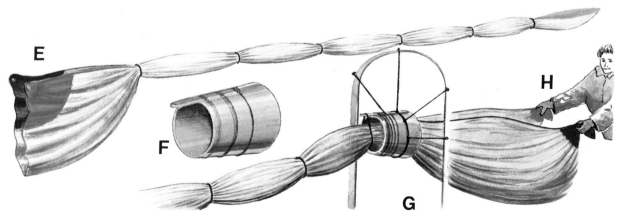

tive it is very difficult to achieve at sea as there is not enough room to lay the spinnaker out. To overcome this an ingenious method has been developed using a plastic bucket with the bottom cut out (**F**).

The bucket is held steady by lanyards and clips attached to its rim, possibly fastened to screw eyes in a door frame as shown in figure **G**. A strip of wood, about ½ inch thick, is glued to the outside of the bucket over which can be stretched a number of elastic bands, the strip enabling these to be picked up easily one by one. As soon as the bucket has been loaded with the bands the head of the sail should be fed through the bucket with another man pulling from the other side (**H**). The person feeding it makes sure that the red and green tapes are together. As the spinnaker is pulled through, an elastic band is pulled off the bucket approximately every 6 feet.

This is a very quick and efficient way of stopping the spinnaker. However there is a great deal of wear and tear on the bucket which needs to be replaced at least twice a year.

Spinnaker sheath

On large yachts, in particular, spinnakers should be set in stops (**J**) or in a sheath. If you try to set straight out of the bag the sail will fill or flog and blow back behind the spreaders, or between the genoa and the mainsail, and this will certainly slow the boat down. A boat travelling at 7 or 8 knots on a reach can drop her speed to as little as 6½ knots.

One way of setting a spinnaker is to have a tubular cover made for it (**K**). This cover should be small at the head, and on one side it should have a zip or velcro strip. To fit the spinnaker staysail inside the sheath start at the head and gradually roll it up from the leech to the luff as you work down towards the foot. If you do this in 6 foot sections you can then put the cover round it and zip it up progressively and it will keep very neat.

When you get to the bottom there should be a tie (**L**) secured to the bottom of the sheath that is clipped to the tack eye of the staysail. Should the bag come off accidentally it will then not blow away. Make sure that the bag is not so long that it covers the clew, which needs to project so that a sheet can be made fast without undoing the sheath. The zip should be fitted so that, when the sheath is completely done up, one side is shorter than the other. Then the sheath is released by pulling down the zip slider until it is only running on the longer part. This allows the other side of the bag to free completely and the sheath will open easily.

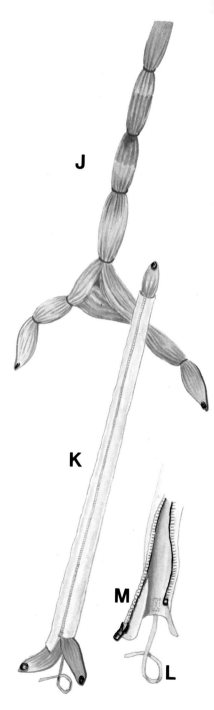

34

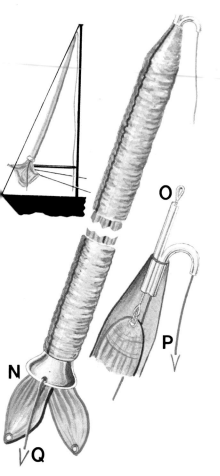

O

P

N

Q

Spinnaker squeeze

A popular method of controlling the spinnaker is by a tube (see diagram). It is well thought out and efficient. Pack the spinnaker by concertinaing the tube up and fastening the head of the spinnaker to the strop inside the top of the tube. Having done this, stretch the spinnaker out and pull the whole sock with its opening down to the bottom of the spinnaker. When the sock is stretched out to its full extent there should be about 12 inches of spinnaker clews left out (**N**).

To set the spinnaker attach the halyard to the eye at the top of the tube (**O**) and hoist away. Make sure that the guy and the sheet are already positioned through the spinnaker pole and attached to the appropriate corner. Then square the pole to the correct angle to the wind and cleat the guy. Haul on the tube halyard (**P**) which pulls the opening up to the top of the spinnaker concertinaing the tube. As it goes up you will find that the spinnaker will start setting and this will help push the tube to the top. You can make the tube halyard double ended and attach it to the bottom (**Q**) so that as

you pull on **P**, **Q** goes up, and you are left with the same amount of rope.

To douse the spinnaker let the spinnaker pole go forward against the forestay and cleat it. Release the spinnaker sheet and pull down hard on **Q**. This will pull the mouth of the tube over the flapping spinnaker until the sail has been totally contained. Once it is inside the tube you can unhook the guy from the corner of the spinnaker guy and pull the tube back to the mast and lower away.

Down wind racing

One of the most exciting moments of my life came when I thought I had achieved the impossible. It happened to me twice, so it was probably not a fluke; once at night and once by day. If beforehand, you had told me that you could gain such a dramatic increase in speed through having the spinnaker, the big-boy and the spinnaker staysail, plus the mainsail all up at once, I would have said you were wrong. But now I know that, if conditions are right, which means an apparent wind speed of 8 to 12 knots and a wind angle of approximately 165°, it is possible to have all these four sails setting and pulling beautifully.

The increase in speed by keeping the spinnaker staysail up was nearly ¾ knot. As you can imagine it was a very exhilarating feeling to have this enormous sail area up and straining to the limits. The speed was so high that, in comparison with the other boats, we might have had our engine on.

I have only been able to do this twice, though I have tried hard to make it work a number of times. The latter occasion was in the 1977 Admiral's Cup when we were running down from Cowes to Portsmouth. *Morning Cloud* and others were catching us up and so we set the spinnaker staysail inside the big-boy and spinnaker and instantly began to move away. It was only a few minutes before the other boats around us noticed what we were doing and followed suit, but we had gained vital distance by being the first to do it and afterwards we held our lead.

Setting the spinnaker

Wind aft

Setting a spinnaker from a pulpit turtle on a run is fairly easy providing some rules are observed (see diagram **A**). These are:

that the packaging has been carried out as advised earlier
that the spinnaker pole is correctly positioned as to height and angle
that the spinnaker guy is tightened so that the clew of the spinnaker is drawn out to the pole end
that the spinnaker turtle is fastened down on the boat

If all these conditions apply, then hoist away until the sail reaches the top, cleat it and then pull on the sheet to break the stops, thus allowing it to fill.

The secret is to fix the pole in the right position and to tighten the foreguy to prevent the pole tipping skywards. If the wind is strong enough to break all the stops too soon, all that will happen is that the spinnaker will flap out forward like a flag.

Follow the sequence through and you will not get into trouble. Problems occur, for example, when the spinnaker sheet is pulled in before the guy has reached the end of the pole, or the pole may not pull aft so that the sail fills to leeward, not only heeling the boat but also putting severe strains on the guy. Then the guy could be pulled out of the crew's

hands leaving the spinnaker half hoisted and streaming from the bow like a kite, but with the guy and sheets slack.

In diagram **B** the same sequence is carried out but this time with a bag that is set on the leeward deck. The main difference is that more spinnaker has to be fed out of the bag to go round the forestay and up to the end of the spinnaker boom. With this method it is better not to pull the spinnaker boom so far aft, but still to set it at its correct height.

Other problems

If the spinnaker will not fill immediately, lower the genoa fast so that the air that the genoa was collecting can then go straight into the spinnaker.

The spinnaker may go up with one or more tight twists in it. One way to clear it is to sheet it as it should be if untwisted and hold it there. The helmsman then has to roll the boat so that the gyrations at the masthead create a twisting movement in the top part of the spinnaker (**C**). Careful observation and timing will usually do the trick.

Twisting around the forestay is more serious and can be obviated by the use of a spinnaker net or a line led back and forth between the forestay and inner forestay (babystay).

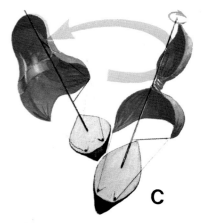

C

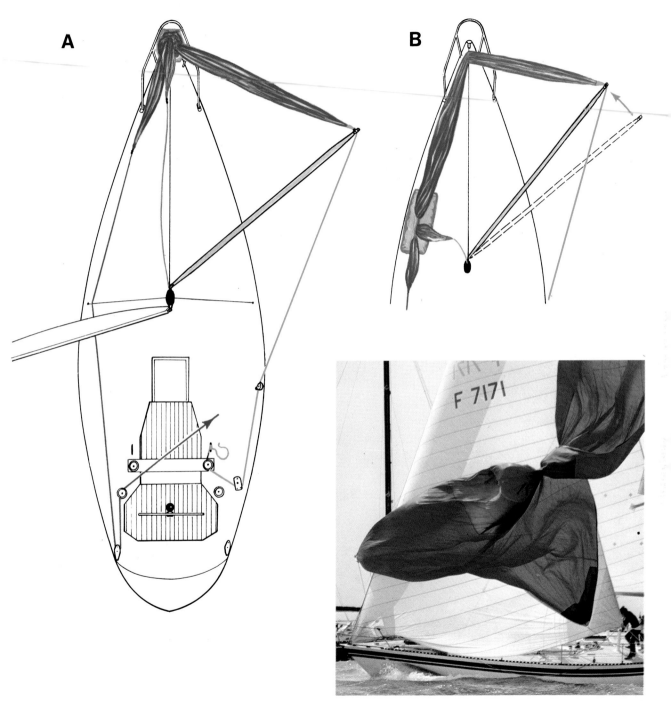

A

B

F 7171

Preparations

Success in setting a spinnaker is almost entirely in the preparation. No matter which system you use always be sure the spinnaker is bagged or stopped correctly (**A**). A point worth remembering when you are stopping a spinnaker is not to place a stop near the head (**a**). This one will be very difficult to break as there is little leverage due to the narrowness of the sail at the top. To break the stops pull sharply on the guy and the sheet together.

When using the sausage bag (**B**) make sure the cringles of the spinnaker are to the appropriate openings of the bag (**b**). Then when taking the bag forward the ties must be fastened securely to the toe rail (**c**). It is essential for these ties to be strong and well secured because it often happens that the bag is on the foredeck for some time before the sail is actually hoisted and a wave could come and wash it over the side. This rule also applies to the pulpit turtle (**C**) although it gets slightly more protection from the forestay which runs down immediately behind it, and also from the pulpit itself which surrounds it.

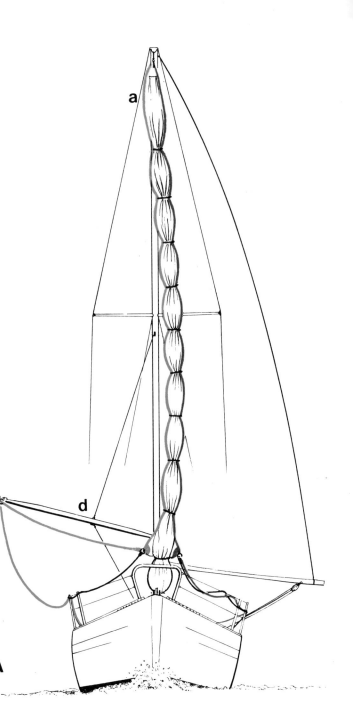

A

40

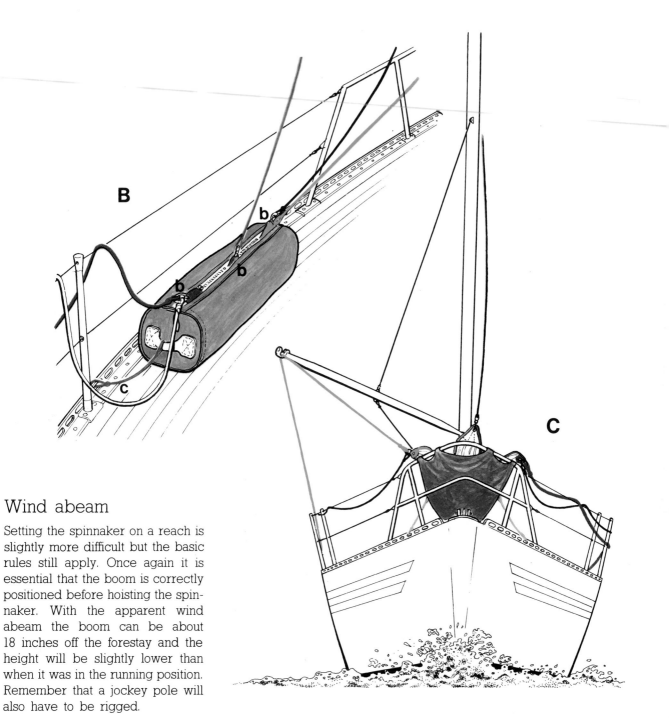

B

Wind abeam

Setting the spinnaker on a reach is slightly more difficult but the basic rules still apply. Once again it is essential that the boom is correctly positioned before hoisting the spinnaker. With the apparent wind abeam the boom can be about 18 inches off the forestay and the height will be slightly lower than when it was in the running position. Remember that a jockey pole will also have to be rigged.

41

When setting from a pulpit turtle (**A**) it is possible to pull just a little of the weather clew out of the turtle and bring it up tight against the spinnaker boom. Then the guy should be turned around a winch, as there will be a heavy strain on it. The reason for the boom being held off the forestay by about 18 inches is that the strain on the guy will make it stretch so that it will then come up against the forestay when the sail is set and drawing.

When the guy has been secured you can hoist away fast on the halyard until the head is at the sheave. When hoisting a spinnaker, the halyard should always be led round a winch so that, if at any time the spinnaker should fill, the halyard will not be torn from the crewman's hand and the spinnaker fall into the sea.

Except on very small boats, two people should hoist a spinnaker. One pulls the halyard down (**a**) and the other tails it round a winch (**b**). It goes up much quicker this way and, should any hitch occur, there is less chance of getting out of control.

Only when the spinnaker is up and the halyard cleated should you haul in on the sheet. This will break

42

open the stops and allow the spinnaker to fill. If the sail is not being set in stops, then the sheet has to be pulled in as the spinnaker is hoisted, but this is naturally harder work all round and there is a greater risk of trouble. If the sheet is not pulled in smartly a twist is likely and this will be very difficult to get out.

As soon as the sail is hoisted, sheeted in and set, and has been checked to see that there are no twists, the genoa should be lowered fast. It is doubtful if the spinnaker will set before the genoa has been doused since, when set and drawing, it bends the air flow but as soon as it does come down you will find that the spinnaker will start filling and the sheet will have to be eased rapidly to avoid overtrimming.

The spinnaker pole and topping lift will have been rigged underneath the weather genoa sheet. When the genoa is lowered the sheets will be seen riding up over the topping lift (near **d** on page 40). When the time comes to lower, it means the genoa sheets remain clear of all spinnaker gear. Plenty of slack must be allowed on the weather genoa sheet for this purpose.

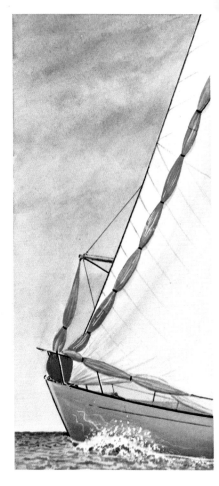

After a gybe, the genoa will be on the wrong side. Then the sheets must be disconnected from the genoa clew, tied together and pulled across the top of the spinnaker topping lift. The genoa is shifted round the foreguy and laid on the new side of the boat. The knotted sheets are brought down on the correct side, and are then reconnected to the clew.

Unless all this is done, the genoa cannot be hoisted on the new gybe,

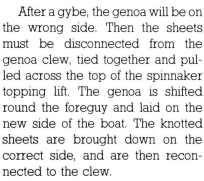

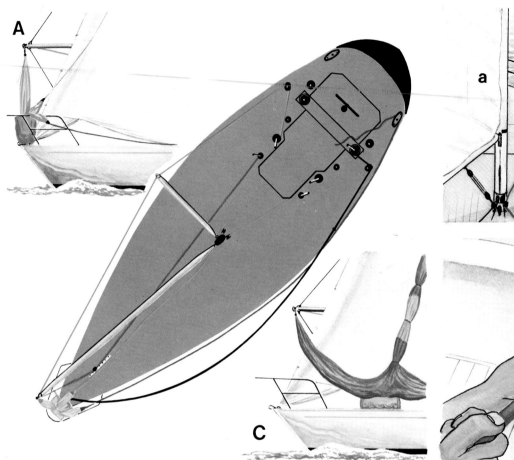

A

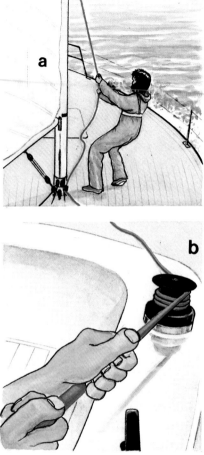

a

b

C

as instructed on pages 76, 78 and 80.

Should the spinnaker have a twist this can usually be removed by lowering the outboard end of the spinnaker pole so that the luff is quite tight, and then hauling down on the leech of the spinnaker.

Often this will untwist the sail quickly, but if the twist is half-way up so that there is an equal amount full of wind above and below, then it is better to lower it immediately, untwist it, and re-hoist. Too much time

can be wasted trying to remove this type of twist.

C shows the method adopted by most of the larger yachts which is a very quick way of setting. Because the bag is fastened to the lee deck, windage is reduced and the turbulence which affects the genoa, arising from the presence of the pulpit turtle, is reduced.

When hoisting the spinnaker this way there is not much need to haul the windward clew out to the end of

the pole because the spinnaker is kept close behind the genoa and it is possible to winch the guy back at the same time as the spinnaker is being hoisted. The sheets should also be tightened just a little to prevent twists. Once the halyard is made fast a little more pulling on the sheet will burst the stops. Then, as in **A**, it is essential to lower the genoa as fast as possible to allow the spinnaker to fill.

Setting the big-boy

Setting a big-boy is in some ways similar to setting a spinnaker, in so far as it has to be pre-packed. The ideal container for this sail is one similar to a spinnaker turtle designed for the pulpit (see page 33, **B**). The big-boy can be packed in exactly the same way as the spinnaker, with the head, tack and clew coming out of their respective openings.

A problem of a big-boy is that the head and tack are very alike and should therefore be marked boldly. It helps to have the clew well marked also. This sail should be set so that it goes up in the lee of the mainsail because it can only be used when the wind is well aft. So I suggest that the bag holding the big-boy should fixed down approximately half-way between the stem and the shrouds on the leeward side. The sheet should be attached to the clew, and taken outside everything to a point near the turning block for the spinnaker sheet, but a little further aft since when the big-boy fills its sheet will be higher than the spinnaker sheet.

A genoa halyard should then be passed over and outside the spinnaker sheet and shackled to the head (make sure again that the bag is fastened down to the rail), then hoist away.

As the sail goes up a crew member can catch hold of the tack and take it forward outside the pulpit and fasten it to the stemhead. Most big-boys have a pendant, approximately 2 feet 6 inches long, on the tack so that it can lift high enough for the helmsman to see underneath. This should be taken to the genoa tack ring, but, if this is just a hook, then I would suggest something a little more permanent. Because of the way the sail is set, and its special cut, it does not have a tight halyard and hence the tack could drop off an open hook.

As a guide you can try easing the halyard approximately 25 per cent of the luff length. You should find that this is just enough to allow the sail to fly out clear of the mainsail and be just above the wave tops when it is full.

Time can be saved by having the big-boy bag just aft of the spinnaker bag. Then attach two halyards and pull the sails up together. This can work very well but I do not recommend it when it is blowing hard!

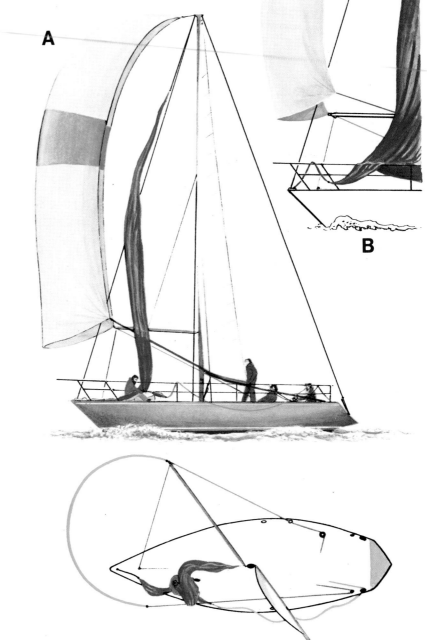

A

B

Setting the spinnaker staysail

When close reaching with the spinnaker set in wind speeds over the deck of 4 knots, it is possible to set the genoa at the same time. On most occasions this will increase boat speed sharply. The handling and trimming of the spinnaker is however far more difficult and critical, so that, on a long offshore leg, it is well worth substituting the spinnaker staysail for the genoa.

This is a sail that is set flying from the masthead and is tacked down 25 per cent of J from the bow. It can be sheeted to the stern, or even to the end of the main boom. An advantage of the latter method is that, when the mainsheet is hauled in, it also tightens the spinnaker staysail sheet.

Most ocean racers fix the tack of a spinnaker staysail a considerable way back from the bow. This is better only in very close reaching. Once the apparent wind is more than 80° off the bow you can progressively move its tack forward and this will greatly increase the speed of the boat. It is easy to see from the drawings just why this should be so since more of the spinnaker staysail is exposed and the centre of effort moves further forward.

I would estimate that you can carry a spinnaker staysail set like this with an apparent wind up to 130° from the bow. From then on you need to set a big-boy instead.

With three-quarter rigs the same things apply but with reduced effect. The genoa can be used for longer periods with advantage, but once the wind has moved aft to abeam the genoa is really no good at all. However, a high-cut genoa that you can sheet to the end of the boom, so getting the clew outboard, is a possibility.

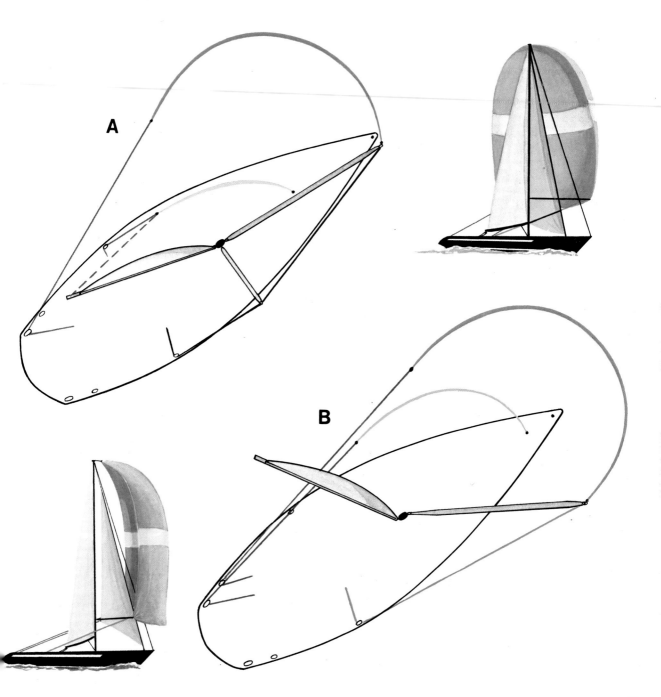

A

B

47

Sail trim

Wind aft – medium and light air

Trimming the spinnaker in these conditions is really quite easy but remember that the pole height is most important in getting maximum pull from the sail. **A** shows the pole too low. The spinnaker has swung out to windward, so that the whole sail has to be pulled aft by the sheet to keep it full of wind. The leading edge, which is on the starboard side, also becomes too full due to the luff tension.

B shows the pole too high which has the opposite effect. The spinnaker swings to leeward which makes the leading edge, again on the starboard side, very flat.

In **C** the pole is at the right height giving evenly balanced edges so that you are able to ease the sheet out a long way (which is what you need to do) before collapsing the sail. When the wind drops the sail will also droop, so the pole has to be dropped too (**D**). Try and keep the outboard end of the pole the same height as the clew of the sail. In very light airs the trimmer can keep the spinnaker full longer if he takes the sheet directly to his hand round the afterside of the mast which makes it set very full (**E**). In more wind the foot of the sail should be spread as much as possible. One method is to

pass the sheet through a snatch block on the outboard end of the boom as in **F**.

Nearly as important as keeping the pole at the right height is the angle of the pole to the wind. Too far forward and the spinnaker becomes very full and can get blanketed behind the mainsail and this encourages rolling (**G**). Too far aft it flattens the sail and so you lose driving force (**H**).

In all winds, except the very light and the very heavy, it is an advantage to ease the spinnaker halyard so that the head of the sail is as much as 2 feet from the sheave. The head can thus move further forward and get into a cleaner airflow away from the forward side of the mast (**J**).

Trim the sheet constantly. First ease out until the windward edge starts curling, then pull in again slowly, then once again let it out. This does two things. It makes sure that the spinnaker is correctly trimmed at all times, on the verge of breaking, and it sets up a bellows effect as it comes in by pumping wind out to leeward. Under the racing rules, you are not allowed to do this for any other purpose than trimming (**K** and **L**).

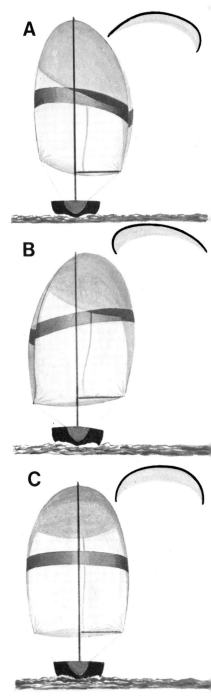

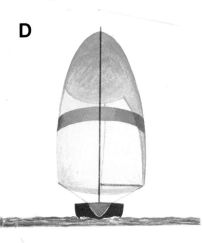

D

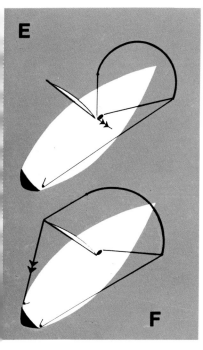

E

F

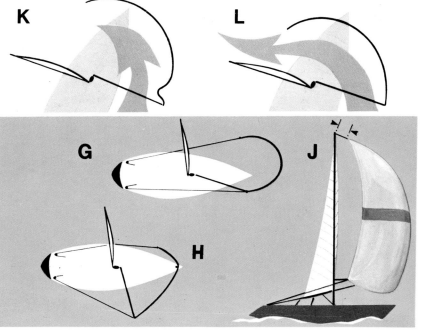

K

L

G

H

J

Wind aft – heavy air

In heavy winds the boat must be as near upright as possible. The angle and height of the spinnaker pole play a very important part in this. As you see from **A**, with the spinnaker pole set too square, the direct pull of the spinnaker is off to port of the boat's track, and this will heel the boat to windward.

B, on the other hand, shows that if a spinnaker pole is too far forward, the pull is to leeward, and so it will cause the boat to heel that way.

C shows the perfect balance between pole angle and sheet tension with the pull of the spinnaker directly forward giving maximum speed. This is the ideal setting, with the wind about 15° from aft.

As for the spinnaker boom height if the outboard end of the pole is too low it makes the luff of the spinnaker too full and the top will swing to windward (**D** and *right*). If it is too high it makes the luff too flat and the spinnaker falls away to leeward as shown in **E**.

It is very important that the spinnaker pole is the right height because if you can keep the boat upright there is less likelihood of a broach. It also reduces the effect of rolling which is covered more fully in the next section.

D

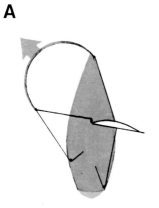

E

A

B

C

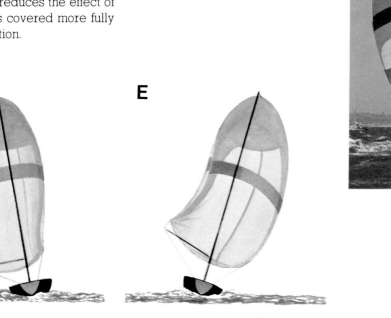

Wind aft – keeping the boat level

To control rolling the pole must first be set at the correct angle (see page 50) and the trimmer must do his job well. If the boat suddenly rolls to windward it is because the sheet has been let out too far, and the pull is therefore in that direction. So winch in the sheet fast to heave the spinnaker back to correct its direction of pull. The masthead will follow the spinnaker, as from **A** to **B**. A leeward roll shows that the sheet is too far in and so ease it immediately. The spinnaker trimmer must concentrate on getting the pull to be from directly forward and an easy way of checking this is to watch the head of the spinnaker in relation to the halyard block. While the pull is directly forward the block is on the centre line. If it starts swinging off to windward it gives the first warning that the sheet wants to come in fast. If it goes to leeward the sheet must go out.

In heavy winds lower the pole somewhat and lead the sheet through a snatch block immediately opposite the mast on the rail. Tied down like this the sail cannot swing from side to side which will help to reduce the rolling (**C** and **D**). The helmsman too should refrain from working too vigorously on the wheel or tiller. He should try to steer with a deliberate movement and, above all, not wind the wheel or move the tiller in time with the rolling (see diagram **E**). If the boat rolls to leeward it will automatically try to luff up. Drastic correction with the rudder causes the water pressure on the rudder actually to help the boat to roll that way so that, when the boat swings back to the other roll and one again corrects it at that point, the momentum will be built up. The effect at high speed can be quite dramatic. Anticipating the rolls, and altering the helm out of phase with them, can often jerk the boat upright.

A big-boy can be a great help in stabilizing the boat. Careful adjustment of the sheets can cause the spinnaker to pull slightly to windward and the big-boy a little to leeward. Balancing these two forces will make the boat very stable, the guy and the big-boy tending to pull the boat straight, thus reducing the amount of steering required (**F**).

Without a big-boy, trim the spinnaker so that it is again pulling a little to windward and bring in the mainsail boom slightly so that the mainsail pull is to leeward. When these are trimmed correctly, it is surprisingly effective in stabilizing the boat (**G**).

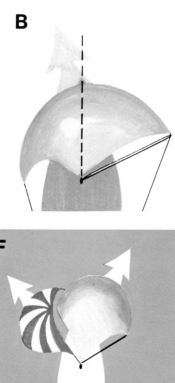

A

B

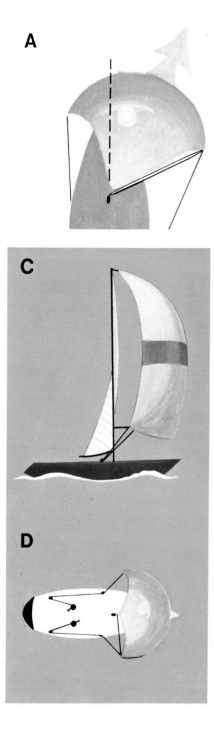

C

D

F

G

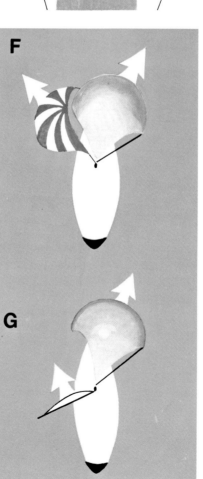

E

Wind abeam – light airs

Reaching in light weather is very difficult and needs close concentration and attention to sail trim.

As usual, the spinnaker boom position is all important. I have sailed many boats with both masthead and three-quarter rig and I have found that with the latter the spinnaker pole must be much higher than with the masthead rig. The smaller mainsail of the masthead rig causes very little problem in maintaining the slot effect, but with the three-quarter rig the overlap of the spinnaker is very much reduced and the slot becomes critical. As you see in drawings **A**, **B** and **C**, it is very noticeable that when you lower the spinnaker halyard sheave (**B**) the spinnaker itself is moved aft at the top compared with the clews. In general to maintain the designed shape you should try to keep the head of the spinnaker at right angles to the line between the two clews so that, when reaching, the pole corner is higher than the sheet corner (**C**).

In drawing **A** note that the spinnaker sheet has been led to a point well forward of the stern so that it bisects the angle of the leech at the foot which, in theory, is correct. However, this is not necessarily best in practice as you can see from **D**, **E** and **F**. If your spinnaker sheet attachment point is forward of the stern it pulls mainly on the leech so that the spinnaker curls too much and there is a hooked flow into the back of the mainsail, so upsetting the slot effect (**D**). If you move the sheet aft, as in **E**, you can see how much more the clew is able to drift out to leeward. The clew of the spinnaker will rise up higher also, but this can be compensated for by adjusting the spinnaker pole height to suit (**F**).

In very light weather it does not pay to set the spinnaker staysail as what little wind there is should be allowed to flow unhindered into the spinnaker.

In a little more wind the helmsman can help to reduce the tendency to broach by bearing away in the puffs and coming up again in the lulls. In very light weather the helmsman can keep up the speed of the boat by doing something similar. The higher the boat can sail the greater the increase in apparent wind speed. This in turn will increase the boat speed and also make the trimming of the spinnaker easier. As the apparent wind increases you can start to bear away again but this has to be done very carefully and very slowly (**G**). Some helmsmen, with a delicate touch, and aided by a sensitive crew, are able to get the boat going much faster than might seem possible in light winds, simply because the boat, by moving forward fast, is generating its own increased wind. Sometimes the boat can sail through patches of no wind at all until it picks up a new wind later on.

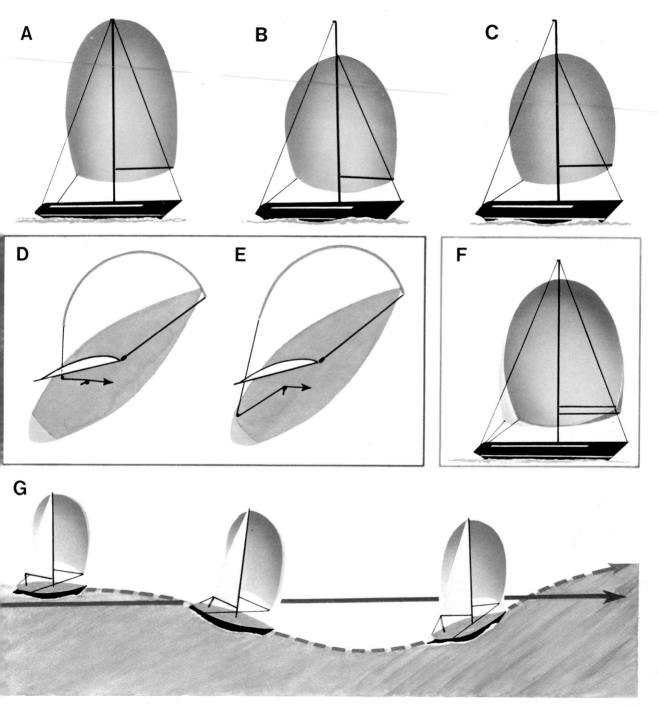

Wind abeam – medium air

For medium wind reaching the spinnaker pole must be kept as nearly at right angles to the apparent wind as possible (**A**) until, when sailing very shy, it reaches a point where it touches the forestay (**B**). Then of course it cannot go any further forward.

The pole height will affect the spinnaker in many ways. The higher it is set, the flatter the sail becomes. There will also be less throwback from the leech of the spinnaker into the mainsail. However, if it goes too high it turns into a mere bubble with little forward drive and only pulls the boat sideways.

I have a good way of finding the correct height of the spinnaker pole which works well if there is sufficient wind to fill the sail properly. Sail the boat as fast as possible with the apparent wind about 60° from the bow. The outboard end of the pole should be adjusted by moving it up first of all, say a foot at a time. Each time the pole is moved up the spinnaker trimmer eases the sheet and notes where the spinnaker lifts first. If it lifts at the bottom first, as in **C**, the pole is too high. If the pole is lowered too much you will find the spinnaker starting to collapse right at the top (**D**). Therefore progres-

sively adjust the pole again until you can get the sail luffing first along the lower two-thirds of its luff as in **E**.

Once you have the correct height it will always be the same for that particular spinnaker, provided the wind is not too light. So the exercise will need to be repeated for each individual sail, as you will need a different pole height for each one. Then mark the mast so that the pole height can be set correctly before hoisting.

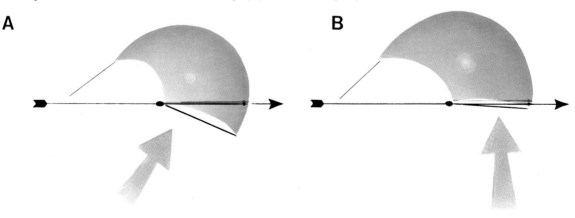

A   B

C

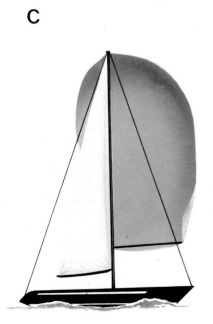

D

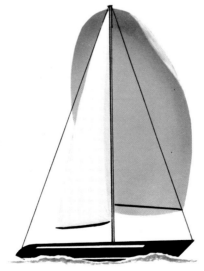

E

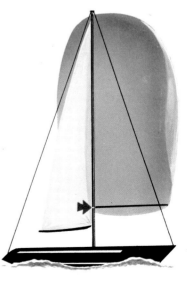

Wind abeam – heavy air

In heavy weather it is best to rig the spinnaker sheet so that it leads over the top of the boom (**A**). This helps in two ways; it opens the slot and allows the spinnaker leech to move further away from the back of the mainsail and it allows you to let the mainsail out in the gusts, as in **B**.

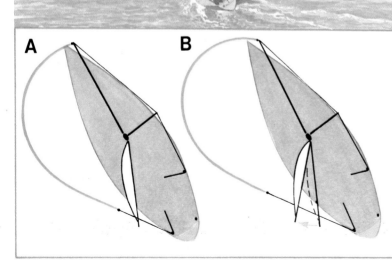

On a reach in strong winds you should steer to the puffs in the same way as was described for light weather, but the course adjustment when a gust hits is far more severe and so the trimming of the spinnaker and mainsail is all important. You must think not only of maintaining speed but also keeping the boat on its feet and avoiding a broach (see pages 72–3).

The big-boy – light to medium air

The big-boy is only really effective with a masthead rig and it is usual to set one with the halyard eased out as far as possible until the foot skims the tops of the waves (**A**). But be very careful when doing this; a crewman should be on the halyard the whole time to hoist it away from the water should it collapse. However, this method is very bad practice and dangerous since you cannot see where you are going. Better to hoist the sail hard up and then adjust the tension with the downhaul. In this way you can still experience some exciting sailing but it will be much safer. Not only can you see where you are going, but it gets the big-boy into an area where there is very little mainsail to disturb the wind flow (**B**).

Too tight a halyard draws the sail in behind the mainsail and starves it of air (**C**).

Having hoisted the big-boy, if there is difficulty in getting it to fill, haul in the mainsheet allowing the wind to go round the back of the mainsail (**F**). Alternatively, the helmsman can luff up slightly allowing the wind to cross the foredeck into the sail. Once it has filled, he puts the boat on to a dead run, or he can even run by the lee.

Some crews reef the mainsail to reduce the area of sail in front of the big-boy (**B**), but providing it is correctly set and trimmed it should work perfectly with a full mainsail.

The big-boy trimmer has a very difficult task, at least until he gets

used to it, since the luff of the big-boy falling in calls for the sheet to be eased, and not to be pulled in as is normal with a headsail (see photograph). Also, if the sheet is eased too much, the luff again falls in so that the trimmer has to be skilled and much practised. Sometimes the leech lifts instead of the luff and this is caused by the sheet being too far in.

The big-boy gets much of its air supply from the spillage off the spinnaker leech. To prove this try setting the big-boy without a spinnaker and you will find it almost impossible. The spinnaker leech should be just aft of the luff of the big-boy as in **E**. Arranged as in **D** a lot of the exhausted air will miss the big-boy altogether.

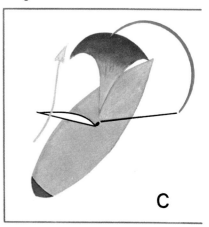

C

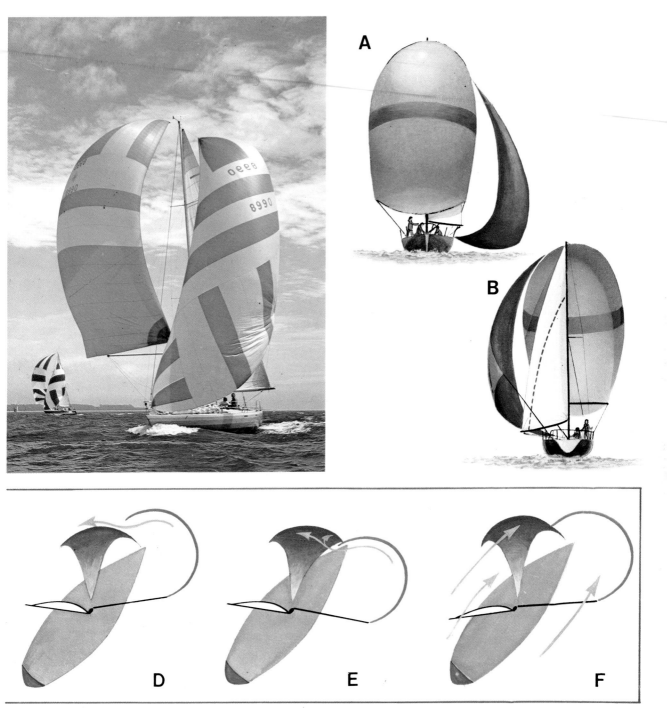

Special reachers – heavy air

Great use can be made of a special reacher on a course which is perhaps a little too close, or a little too windy, to set the spinnaker. This is a sail with a full length luff, and the same LP as the genoa, but which is high clewed.

A genoa's clew comes very near the sheet lead (see **A**) so that when you ease the sheet there is a tremendous pull-back on the clew causing it to curl in excessively on the foot.

The reacher is high clewed, as in **B**. The distance from the clew to the sheet lead is far greater and the clew can drift out away from the back of the mainsail. This gives more driving power, less heeling moment and a wider slot so that the mainsail can be let out further without being backwinded. This again reduces heeling moment and gives more driving force and reduces weather helm.

Furthermore, because the clew of the reacher is able to drift further out away from the mainsail it is possible to set a reefed spinnaker staysail inside, as in **C**. This is an excellent rig when it is blowing hard, and especially so when the mainsail is reefed. It is possible to set a tall-boy or slotsail instead of the reefed spinnaker staysail, but this is not so effective (**D**).

When reaching in a blow you often see yachts with two or three reefs in the mainsail, together with either a full genoa, or a full reacher (**E**). This is the wrong rig to use in these conditions. Better to have a full hoist no 2 or even a no 3 and shake out the reefs, as in F. This rig will also reduce the amount of weather helm allowing you to reach faster.

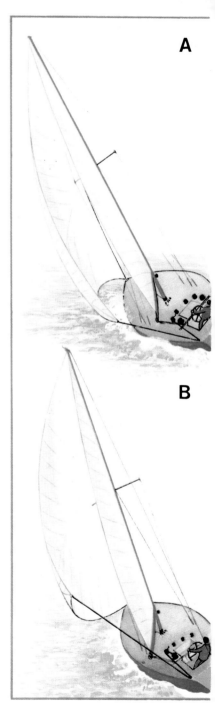

A

B

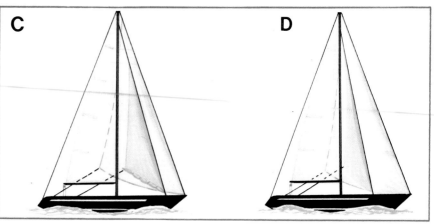

C

D

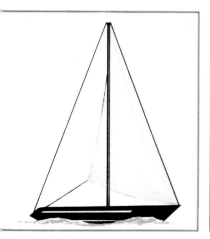

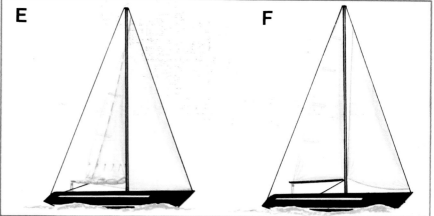

E

F

63

Trimming the mainsail

Shape

Figure **A** shows a typical section of a mainsail when sailing to windward with the clew hauled out to the measurement mark. The normal action when starting a downwind leg is to ease the outhaul to make the sail fuller. This gives it more pulling power (**B**), but also reduces the projected area (**D**) of the sail. However if the foot is eased from the tack end, it results in the same increase in curvature (**C**) with the extra advantages that it loosens the luff, shifts the centre curvature aft and makes the sail very baggy (**E**) while still retaining maximum projected area.

Figure **F** shows a close-up of this arrangement. Note that the sail entries on the boom and the mast have to be well away from the tack fitting to allow an easy angle for the roping or track.

Whatever system is used, one thing to ensure is that the luff is not too tight. An over-tensioned luff off the wind will give the mainsail a section similar to that in **G**, whereas it should be more like **H**. For sails not fitted with a cunningham hole to let go the tack, ease off the main halyard instead. The end of the boom will droop (**J**) but the sectional shape of the sail is more important.

Twist in the mainsail should be controlled with care, but is often ignored. In theory the airfoil ought to be in one plane (*left*) but most boats appear to go faster when the mainsail is allowed to twist off a little (*right*). There is no easy guide as to how much to allow. I allow more in light winds and increase it gradually until I find I am going fast and then hold it there.

In light airs you can attach a topping lift to the end of the boom to take the weight and then tension it against the kicking strap. Modern ocean racers can hold the boom up on a solid or hydraulic kicking strap.

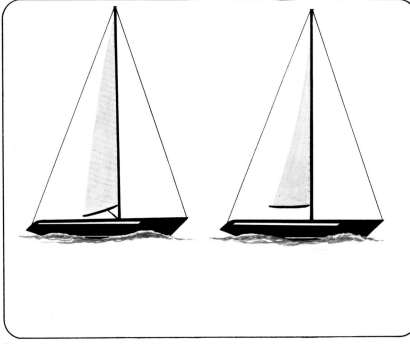

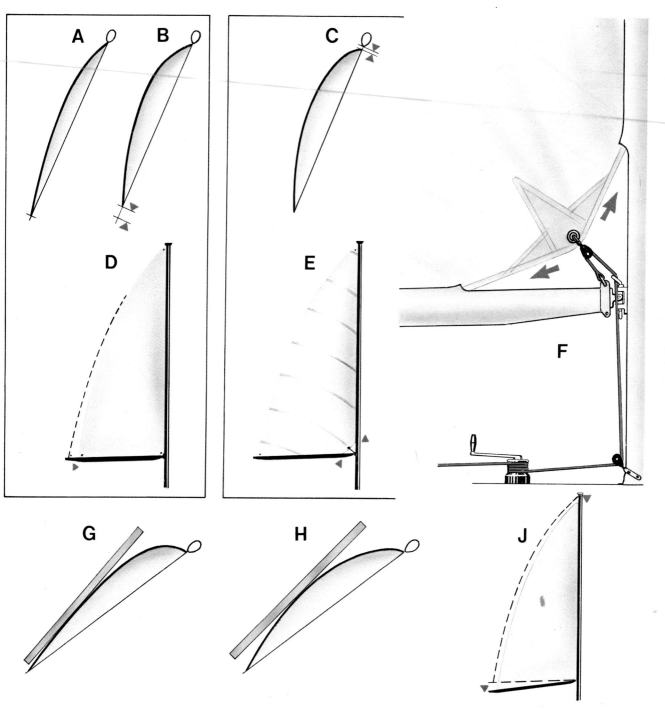

Boom vangs and kicking straps

The device which leads from the boom to the base of the mast at the deck is called a kicking strap in Britain, but in other parts of the world, including the USA, it is called a boom vang. In Britain this latter word is reserved for the tackle which holds the boom out and forward to the rail against the pull of mainsheet. It is a very useful device in light weather, or when the boat is rolling violently, and will deter an involuntary gybe, but it can cause serious trouble in the event of a leeward broach and subsequent gybe.

A shows a vang taken from the bottom of the boom down to the toe rail. If the fall of the tackle goes to a winch near the mainsheet trimmer he can adjust it as well as the mainsheet.

Four of the most common kicking strap systems are shown here. **B** is the system which acts rather like a rigging screw, with a very coarse thread at either end and an operating wheel. The female nut at the lower end slides within the tube against a spring so that you can tighten the mainsheet without adjusting the wheel each time. In light weather there is sufficient strength in the spring to take the weight of the boom, and so build up the necessary twist mentioned on the previous page.

C is a simple push/pull hydraulic ram controlled from the cockpit. The two exposed pipes at the base of the ram have always worried me. I have nightmares that something will catch on them and break them off. Then there would be hydraulic oil over everything – and no kicking strap!

D is the simplest, being just a block and tackle which can either be jammed off at the lower block or taken to a winch. This is often used in small boats and holds the boom down well but in light airs, when you want to take the weight of the boom, a topping lift would have to be used.

E is the latest big-boat gadget which has been developed from the dinghy classes. It is compact, with low friction, and the lever can give enormous power for very little expense. Again you need a topping lift to take the weight of the boom in light weather.

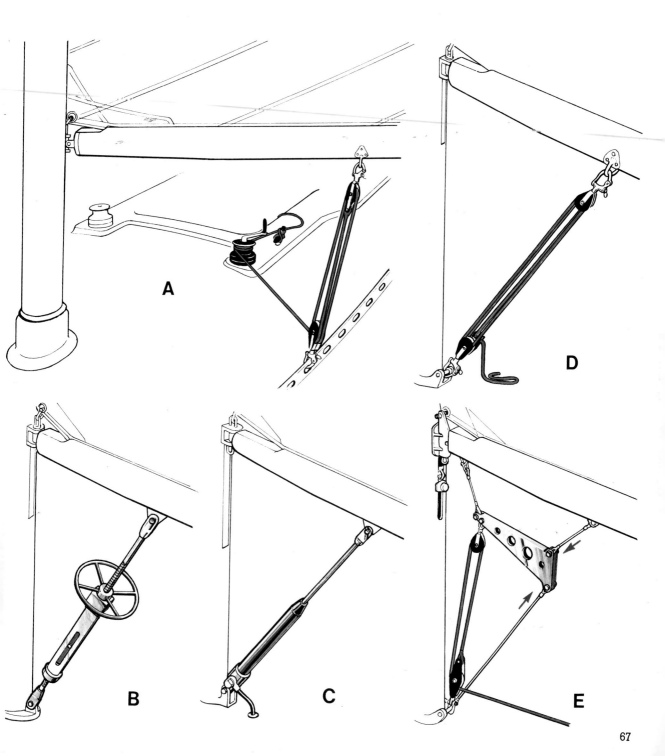

A

B

C

D

E

Trimming the boat – balance and heeling

Boat trim is just as important as sail trim. Figure **A** shows how, in light weather on a dead run, you should try to heel the boat slightly to windward, thus allowing the spinnaker to swing to windward so catching all the air that is going past the mainsail. It also raises the boom slightly which moves more of the mainsail up into faster-moving air.

On the other hand, when reaching in light weather, keep the spinnaker and mainsail full by heeling the boat to leeward so that the spinnaker hangs out as far to leeward as possible and allows gravity to help the mainsail take up a natural shape (**B**). Heeling to leeward is also essential if you are carrying a light reacher or drifter. Again the gravity effect on the sail pulls it into the correct shape (**C**).

Heeling also has the effect of slightly reducing the wetted surface, thus giving less drag. Similarly, on a run in light weather it is well worth trimming the boat down by the bow (**D**). This lifts the wider aft sections out of the water and effectively increases the forward rake of the mast. All of this is good for speed.

In heavy weather, to ensure complete control of the boat, move all crew weight right aft. This stops the bow digging in, allows the flat aft sections to take more load and also keeps the rudder as deep as possible (**E** and photograph).

A

B

C

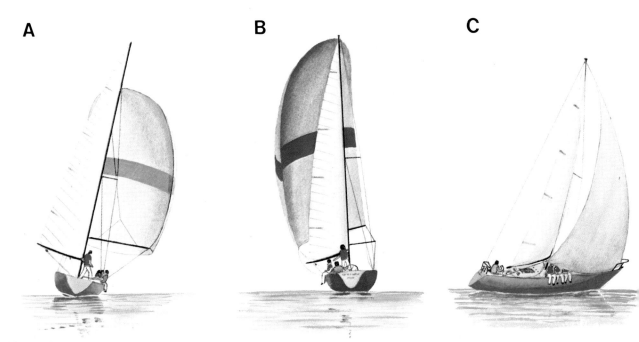

D

E

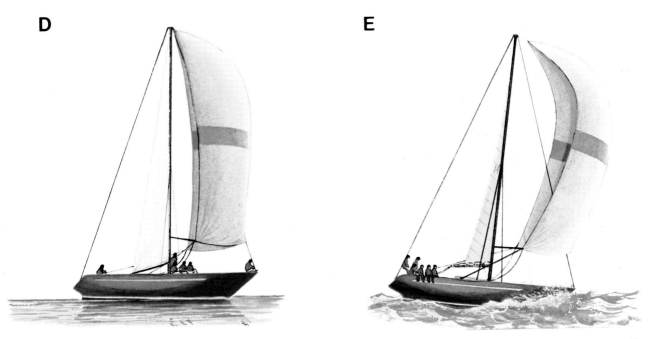

The broach to windward

The dynamics of a wipe-out

A broach is caused by the forces acting on the rig and hull trying to turn the yacht, and then overcoming the corrective force exerted by the rudder.

In a broach to windward, the boat heels in a gust, or on a wave, and the forward driving force on the rig is displaced to one side of the line of forward progress of the boat, forming a turning moment (**A**). The keel area increases this with its 'tripping-up' action. The rudder (**B**) lifts the stern, making matters even worse, and stalls out. The boat starts to swing uncontrollably, aided by the centrifugal force of the mast and rig. The disaster is completed by the pressure of wind in the mainsail which cannot swing out as the boom-end is dragging in the water.

The photographs (*below*) show a straightforward mild broach and recovery.

Prevention

In hard weather excessive broaching loses distance and also puts a great deal of strain on the gear, so how can a broach be prevented?

If your boat's mast can be raked fore and aft, it should be moved as far forward as possible (**A** to **B**) to shift the centre of effort forward.

The boat that is fitted with a very easily adjustable kicking strap (vang) can 'scandalize' the mainsail by releasing the vang in a heavy gust just before a broach can begin (**C**). This moves the centre of effort forward quickly, and can be very effective. Even if the release of the vang is left a little too late it will make the broach a mild affair.

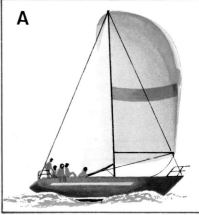

A

C

Moving the crew weight aft also reduces the broaching tendency by lifting the bow and keeping the stern well down so that the rudder is more effective (**D**). Yet another preventative is to set an additional headsail up forward. The extra area ahead of the mast can help to push the bow to leeward before the broach can take charge (see page 75, *bottom right*).

In heavy conditions the helmsman should watch for gusts approaching. As the ruffled water caused by the strong gust is about to hit the boat, bear away sharply and sail with it (**E**). As the gust dies away, then luff up (**F**). The change of course should not be too violent. You will find that you will not have to alter the sheets since the increase in wind speed when the gust strikes, and the increase in the speed of the boat, will bring the apparent wind further ahead.

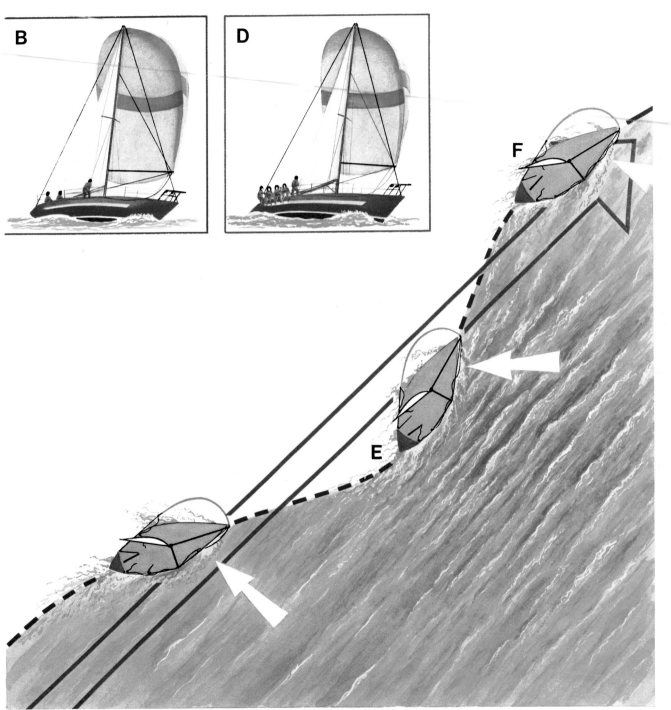

B

D

F

E

73

The broach to leeward

Getting back on course

The worst type of situation arises after a leeward broach and subsequent gybe when the mainsail boom has been bowsed down to the rail and is now held vertically in the air by the vang. The wind catches the mainsail aback and presses the boat down flat. Obviously the vang must be released, or cut free, fast! A boat may even fill through the main hatch if this is not attended to. As the boat comes upright there is likely to be a massive tangle to unwind, and possibly some damage too.

After a bad leeward broach the boat may refuse to come up more than half-way and cannot be made to bear away. You can waste a lot of time if you do not know what to do.

The trouble is caused by the clew area of the mainsail which is dragging in the water. As soon as the boat comes up the mainsail fills, the boat gathers way, the water pushes the

main boom aft (thus sheeting in the sail) and the wind pushes the boat over again. Back to the beginning again! This can go on for ever.

The cure is to reduce wind pressure aft of the mast, so let go the kicking strap (vang); the boom lifts, freeing the wind out of the sail, and the boat will come up. Bear away, re-set the spinnaker and carry on sailing. In an emergency the spinnaker halyard might be let go.

I find that it is worth setting a headsail of some type in addition to the spinnaker when broaching is likely. Not only does this increase the amount of sail forward of the mast, but if a violent broach occurs, by sheeting in the headsail the boat will often pay off again.

Down spinnaker

With the wind aft

Lowering the spinnaker on a run can produce problems even for the most experienced crews. In most cases it is just lack of team work that is the cause of the trouble.

After hoisting the genoa on the right side (see page 42) one man should go forward to the pulpit and the person on the guy allows the spinnaker boom to go right forward until it is up against the forestay. Do not forget to tighten the foreguy at the same time to keep the boom under control (**A**). Then cleat the guy and lower the spinnaker pole lift until the man standing in the bow can reach the tripping line on the snap shackle on the end of guy. Then cleat the lift.

Before releasing the spinnaker at the guy end, the man in the pulpit must make absolutely sure that the crew on the sheet is ready to haul in the sail foot the moment he lets go. Then he can undo the clip and let the spinnaker fly out forward like a flag (*right*). The sail should now present no problem as there is very little weight in it. It is only a matter of the man who was up forward coming back to help haul down the spinnaker behind the mainsail (**B** and *bottom centre*).

The crew originally on the guy and the lift can then ease the halyard carefully, not faster than it can be pulled in or it will blow forward and catch the wind (**C**) or end up under the bow.

When there is a lot of wind it is difficult for the crew to hear reliably, so one man should stand by the shrouds telling each member of the crew exactly what he wants done. This way you might avoid the problem that often happens when the halyard is let go at the same time as the guy and in the panic the sheet is let go too and the sail flies out forward. It really is remarkable just how often spinnakers can be seen in this embarrassing position after turning the lee mark (*bottom right*).

A

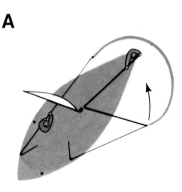

B

C

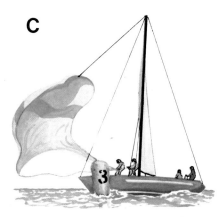

With the wind abeam

The same method is used for a reaching drop, but the forces involved, especially in a breeze, are much greater and therefore more care has to be taken.

First set the genoa so it is ready to trim for the next leg of the course, or for the change in wind that has necessitated dropping the spinnaker. It also blankets the spinnaker, as the latter is lowered.

Take the bight of the lazy guy over the life line and under the main boom and into the centre of the yacht, or in the hatch. One or more crew will use this to haul in the spinnaker clew. Especially on bigger boats, rig a snatch block and a line on to the spinnaker sheet to enable it to be hauled in via another snatch block on the toe rail (**B**). When ready to drop, make absolutely certain the spinnaker sheet is cleated (**C**), then lower the spinnaker boom to a height that the crew member up forward can reach. This man is in control, and so when he has established that everybody is ready he can trip the guy snap shackle at the end of the spinnaker boom (*left*). When doing this he must not stand to windward of the boom because there is a sharp reaction from the spinnaker boom once the tension is released which could knock him overboard.

A

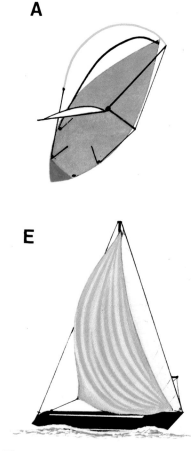

E

The spinnaker is now flying out to leeward like a flag (*right*) and the tail of the snatch block on the sheet should be winched in hard (**D**). In moderate winds this can probably be done by hand. Having caught hold of the spinnaker sheet the halyard can be eased away slowly. The vertical edge of the spinnaker must be kept fairly tight. Once this gets slack the sail can flog and can be pulled out from the crew's hand.

Another way of getting in the spinnaker on a reach is to attach a downhaul on to the tack. Take this through a snatch block on the stemhead, and then to a winch. By tightening up on this line, at the same time easing out on the guy, you can pull the tack of the spinnaker down on to the stemhead. At the same time tighten up on the sheet so that the foot of the spinnaker is lying alongside the lifeline. Then the crew members can lean under the genoa and haul it down while the halyard is being slacked away (**E**).

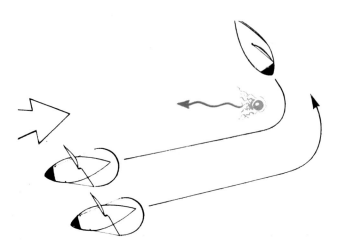

A flying drop

A flying drop, or a gybe-and-drop, is only for use when racing. When running down to a mark against the tide you may need to gybe at the last minute and then the use of this technique may gain many places.

First hoist the genoa (**A**) in plenty of time. It does not blanket the spinnaker too much when on a dead run, providing it is held nearly amidships. On approaching the mark trip the spinnaker boom from the guy and allow it to swing in as if you were gybing with a dipped pole. The spinnaker should then be trimmed with the two sheets and, if the wind is dead aft, it will minimize the difficulty in doing this (**B**).

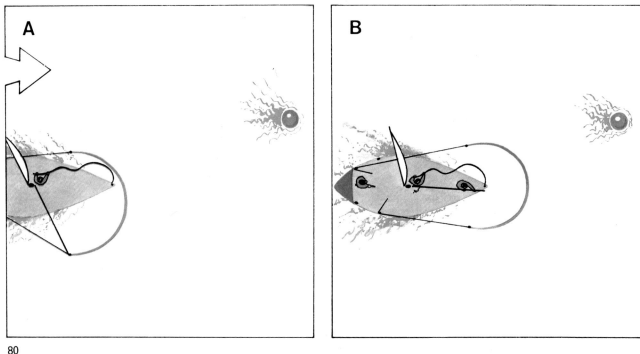

A

B

The release of the spinnaker boom from the spinnaker has to be judged carefully because, under the racing rules, you may not sail for any length of time without a boom being attached. Once it has been stowed away on the foredeck the boat must be ready to round the mark and can then be gybed (**C**).

Assuming a port hand rounding, the guy (starboard side) is pulled in and, as the boat starts to round, the guy and sheet (port side) are let go so that the spinnaker flies out to leeward. Then it can be pulled down, starting at the 'guy' corner (**D**).

On all points of sailing there can be an advantage in the use of a retrieving line in the centre of the sail, especially if a spinnaker tube is used for stowing below deck.

C

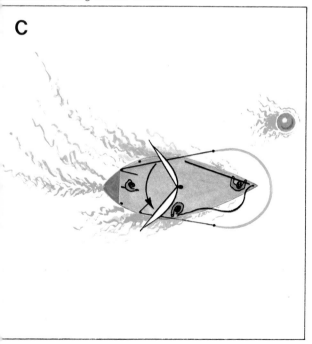

D

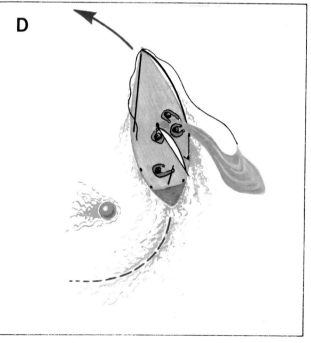

Down big-boy

Lowering a big-boy really presents no difficulty at all providing you take the wind out of it and keep it under control.

I have found the best way to lower the big-boy is first to release the clew from the sheet or to let the sheet go altogether so that the sail is flying out ahead of the boat as in figure **A**. Then a crew member should get hold of the tack and run this back to the base of the mast so that it is partly hidden by the mainsail (**B**). This man can then gather the sail as the halyard is eased off.

The crew on the halyard has to watch that he does not ease off so fast that the luff of the big-boy goes slack. So many times when a big-boy is being lowered the person on the halyard becomes impatient and eases out too soon. The sail simply blows out forward into the water (**C**).

There is one other way of lowering this sail by letting go the tack. The crew catches hold of the sheet and takes it forward pulling it down clew first (**D**). It works reasonably well, but the tack end, being lower than the clew, often falls into the

water and can get dragged underneath the bow.

A spinnaker staysail is just a simple. Just let go the sheet so that all the wind is taken out of the sai and then gather it in as quickly a possible on to the foredeck. It i essential when racing that this sa comes down fairly fast becaus there is nothing that slows you speed more than a spinnake staysail that is not pulling properl In fact, the faster any sail is lowere the less chance there is of it gettin out of control.

Gybing

The gear required

Start by gybing a spinnaker from one run to the other. Compared with gybing from a reach to a reach this is easy. There is plenty of time and the change of angle is small. The success of this operation is essentially a team venture with the helmsman playing a major part.

A shows the set-up for a twin-pole gybe which can be used in any size boat. It is ideally suited for when it is blowing very hard since the spinnaker is under close control the whole time. However it is a very cumbersome method and needs an extra pole and track.

B1 and **B2** show a boat rigged for a dip-pole gybe which is extremely quick, needs no extra equipment but does need exceptional team work and careful timing. The success or failure of this type of gybe depends mainly on the helmsman following the spinnaker so that it does not collapse, and the crew member in the pulpit to pulling the pole inboard and clipping in the new guy fast.

C is for smaller boats which are the only ones that can use the end-for-end gybe. This method needs only one sheet on either corner of the spinnaker and therefore cut down the cost even more than B. However a 25 foot boat is about the largest in which one can do this safely.

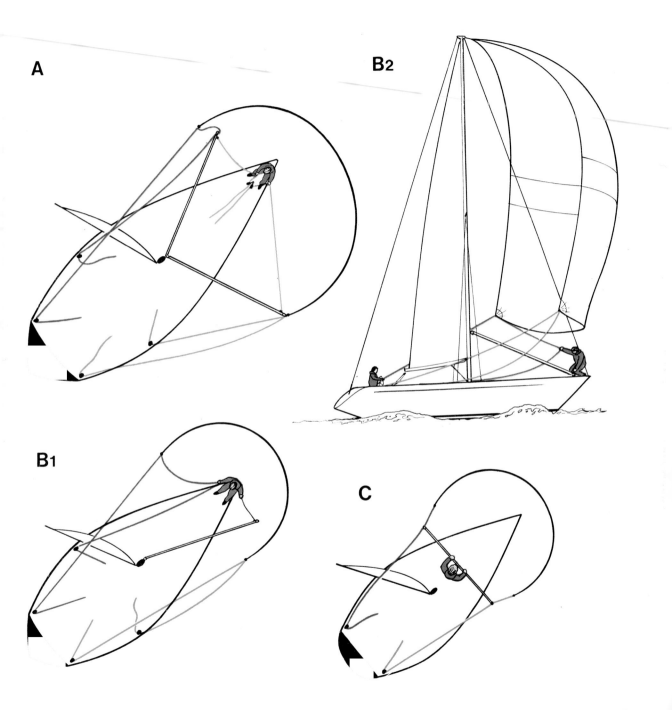

A

B2

B1

C

The twin-pole gybe

You can rig the second pole some time before actually gybing. It can be fitted into a second slide on the spinnaker pole track and the inboard end hoisted up to the level of the pole in use. The forward end can be left on the foredeck inside the lifelines and it can stay in this position until required (**A**).

The sequence thereafter is as follows:

1. Take the bight of the new (lazy) guy and clip it through the end of the new spinnaker pole so that it leads from the spinnaker from starboard to port (when on starboard tack).
2. Hoist the new pole to the same level as the one in use, and cleat off the lift.

3. Tighten the lazy guy to pull the new pole end out to the spinnaker corner – just tight enough to make the sheet go slightly slack. Then cleat the guy and the boat is ready to gybe.
4. To start the gybe adjust both poles to about 45° from the bow. Then gybe the main boom and trim the mainsail.

5. Take up the strain on the new sheet and ease off the old guy a long way. The bowman pulls in on the foreguy to bring the pole inboard.
6. With the old pole end on the deck, the bowman unclips the old guy, which is then tightened until it is just clear of the water. Unship and stow the pole; adjust the new pole height and angle, and trim the sheets.

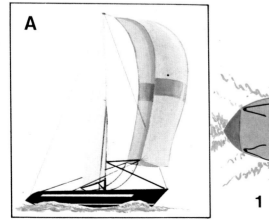

A

1

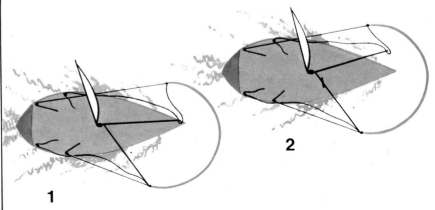

2

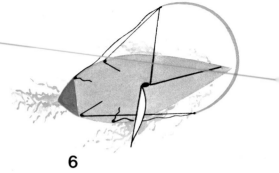

6

Problems

If you try to gybe with the poles still squared aft (position 4), the spinnaker will be pulled tight across the forestay. This could tear the sail and in any case will slow the boat. In heavy weather it will also end up by causing a broach (**B**).

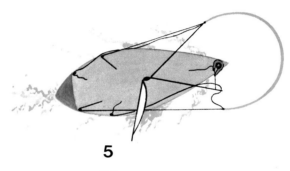

5

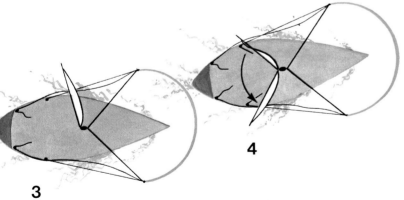

3

4

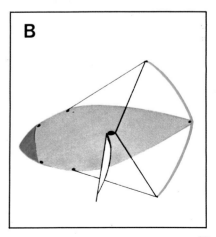

B

The dip-pole gybe

Single-pole or dip-pole gybing are very efficient, but they need close team work and careful preparation. On the mooring, first mark the mast where the spinnaker pole slider has to be positioned before starting a gybe. It has to be high enough to enable the outboard end of the pole to pass clear astern of the forestay when it is dipped. The mark should be all the way round the mast so that the crew can see it from any part of the boat. Then mark the spinnaker pole lift where the lift operator can see it, and so that it corresponds with another on the deck when the spinnaker boom lift is dipped the correct amount (**A**).

Each crewman must be allocated his job; one on the spinnaker pole lift and to release the guy, a second up forward to pass the end of the pole behind the forestay and attach it to the new guy. One or two more must work the sheets and guys. Probably the most important job is the helmsman's. He has to steer the boat far enough off the wind so that the spinnaker is positioned dead ahead of the boat. Only when he is satisfied that he can hold the spinnaker there, and the boat has stopped rolling, can he start to gybe. He calls 'gybe-ho!' and the pole is released from the old

guy. The spinnaker is now held only by both sheets and it is up to the helmsman to ensure that it does not start to swing or, worse still, collapse.

So the sequence is like this:

1 Slack off the new (lazy) guy and take the bight forward to the pulpit. The bowman takes it and sits in the pulpit, forward of the forestay, facing aft. He also grasps the spinnaker pole foreguy and calls out, 'Ready to gybe!'
2 Helmsman steers the boat straight down wind and calls 'Gybe-ho!' Crewman by the mast pulls the trip line to release the guy and raises the pole lift to the predetermined mark. The man on the starboard winches transfers the spinnaker load on to the new sheet. Bowman pulls the pole to him with the foreguy and clips the new guy into the pole end. Mainsheet tender starts hauling in the mainsail.
3 Bowman throws the pole end outboard. Crewman by the mast lowers the pole end quickly. Mainsheet hand gybes the mainsail.

4 Almost simultaneously the man on the port winches heaves in on the new guy, adjusts the boom angle and releases the old sheet.

The important part that the helmsman plays in this operation is as follows:

bear away on to a dead run
stabilize the boat with the spinnaker always dead ahead
as soon as the spinnaker pole is across the centre line, and as the mainsail is passing across the deck, bear away slightly (with reference to the new gybe)
turn gradually to final course

Notes

Try to keep the main boom in line with the spinnaker boom (ie they both come inboard and pass the centre line together).

Larger or smaller boats may have more or fewer people to do the various jobs. The exact duties of each must be worked out in advance.

Done correctly this can be a very slick operation but in some modern boats with very large rigs, and in hard winds, the tendency to rolling may dictate the safer but clumsier twin-pole method.

A

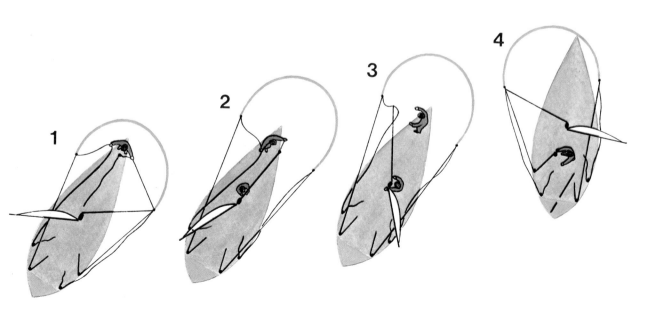

1   2   3   4

The end-for-end method

For a small boat of, say, up to 26 feet with a masthead rig (or 30 feet when three-quarter rigged) it is simplest and cheapest to use the end-for-end method. The spinnaker pole is identical at both ends. The mast end is unclipped, the pole is passed across and attached on the other side. You can gybe quickly and efficiently this way but, like everything else, it is the technique plus perfect team work between helmsman and the man on the pole which makes for success.

In more detail, a starboard to port gybe goes as follows:

1 The helmsman steadies the boat. The crew eases the downhaul to make it easier to unclip and clip on again.
2 The crew faces forward and unhooks the pole end from the mast.

3 The helmsman brings the spinnaker sheet near the boat by bearing away slightly, or by grabbing the sheet and pulling it sideways. The crew walks sideways and catches the sheet while still holding the pole, which is hanging from its topping lift; he then connects the sheet, which becomes the new guy, and calls 'Pole connected!'

1

2

3

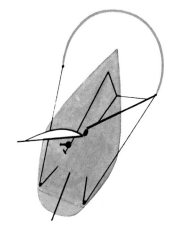
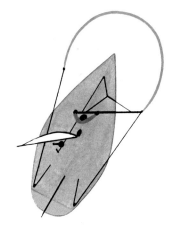
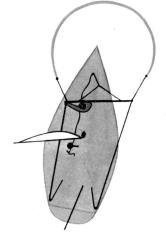

4 The helmsman bears away slightly and starts pulling in on the mainsheet. The crew moves to the centre line and holds the pole horizontal by its middle.

5 The helmsman gybes the mainsail. The crew moves to starboard, pushes the pole out to port and unhooks the old guy (new sheet). The helmsman lets out the mainsail and steadies the boat, bearing away slightly if necessary.

6 The crew pushes the pole out fully, moving across the boat, then clips the pole end on to the mast, tightens the downhaul and moves aft to adjust the sheet and guy.

Points to note

The helmsman must steer accurately to keep the boat at the right angle to the wind and to help the crew.

After the gybe the boat must not be luffed too fast. In fresh winds this will lead to a broach with the pole still not connected (see photograph on page 99).

Alternative method

You can gybe the pole before gybing the mainsail. The advantage is that the crew can then come aft sooner to trim the sheets, and the spinnaker is fully connected at the moment of gybing. This works best in plenty of wind otherwise the spinnaker can collapse behind the mainsail and perhaps become wrapped.

4

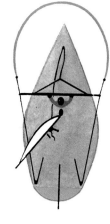

5

6

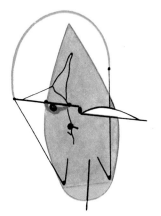

From a reach to a reach

Gybing a spinnaker from a reach to a reach is only done when racing. The cruising man has all the time in the world and can always make his gybe from a run to a run. However the racing man will often have to reach up to a mark on one gybe, round the mark and then reach off on the other gybe. Unless it can be done slickly he can lose a lot of valuable time and get into a muddle. As usual, perfect team work within the crew is essential.

It is vital, first of all, that the helmsman positions the boat correctly, making sure that he only turns in time with the speed that his crew can handle the gear, while going through the manoeuvre. Some crews are faster than others and the helmsman must then gybe more quickly or he will find himself in just as much trouble as if he had moved the boat too fast for a slow crew.

The tactic on gybing at a reaching mark is to be as close to it as possible and going fast when going away. This stops other competitors getting between you and the buoy and also, if anyone has left a gap, you will immediately overtake without problem.

The dip-pole method

This is the most straightforward method and so I will describe it first.

There are two alternative approach tracks shown in figure **A**. The blue track is not to be recommended since you cannot gybe until the mark is passed and the boat will therefore end up well to leeward when on the new course. The brown track is best and is here keyed to the sequence of manoeuvres shown in the other diagrams. This track starts well to windward and the gybe occurs at, or even a little before, the mark. The 'two lengths' rule protects you from intruding boats but, even if another boat came up from leeward and passed ahead before the mark, you would still end up in front of her thereafter.

The approach track has to be gauged with wind angle and current in mind so that the boat is on a dead run just before reaching the mark.

So the boat starts with the pole on the forestay and jockey pole in place:

1 Start easing the sheets and bearing away slowly.

2 Bear away faster, pull the spinnaker pole aft and ease the spinnaker sheet.

3 Put the boat on to a dead run, fully ease the sheet, square the pole aft and steady the boat.

4 The secret is to make sure that the sheet is fully eased out and the pole pulled right aft. Then trip the pole end from the guy and re-connect it to the new guy and then gybe the mainsail. Only pull the pole a couple feet or so back off the forestay.

5 Fit the jockey pole, haul in fast on the sheet and then start luffing up. The strain on the guy will stretch it so that it may hardly need to be eased at all.

6 Finally trim and adjust the sails to be moving fast on the new course only just to leeward of the mark and well to windward of the other boats.

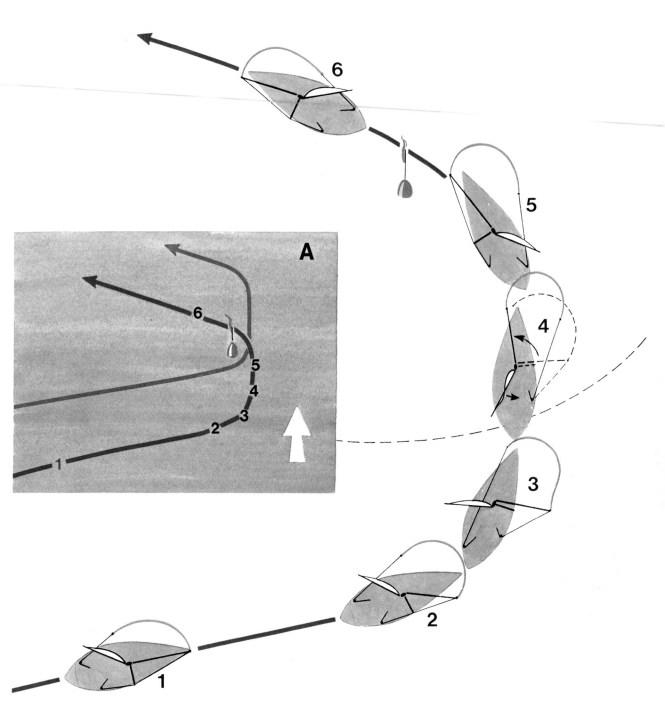

The end-for-end method

Using the end-for-end method the helmsman should still follow the recommended course, keeping well to windward on the approach. The general principles and timings are the same. Start easing off the sheet and bearing away as at positions 1 and 2 above, at the same time squaring off the pole. Then:

3 Bear away more quickly on to a dead run when the sheet should be fully eased and the pole right back. Again beware that the snap shackle has not actually touched the forestay and unclipped itself. An additional job at this time is to ease a foot or so of downhaul or topping lift.

4 Steady the boat. The crew, facing forward, unclips the pole at the mast end, moves across the boat and clips it on to the old sheet (new guy) which has been pulled in by the helmsman or another crewman. Immediately, he thrusts the pole outboard and forward (on no account must he pull the pole aft) and calls out 'Pole clipped on'.

5 The helmsman bears away a little and pulls the mainsail amidships, then gybes. The crew unclips the pole from the old guy and clips the end on to the mast.

6 Tighten the downhaul. Keep the pole end near the forestay and slowly luff up, hauling in the sheet steadily. The aim is to shave the mark with full speed and full control so that no other boat can get further to weather.

Yet again it is team work and practice that produce the results. It is well worth trying the manoeuvre again and again on a practice mark a little faster each time. But in a real race the helmsman must gauge his turn exactly to the speed of the crew, not going on to the next stage until the last is completed. He must hold the boat on a dead run long enough for all the essential movements to be finished.

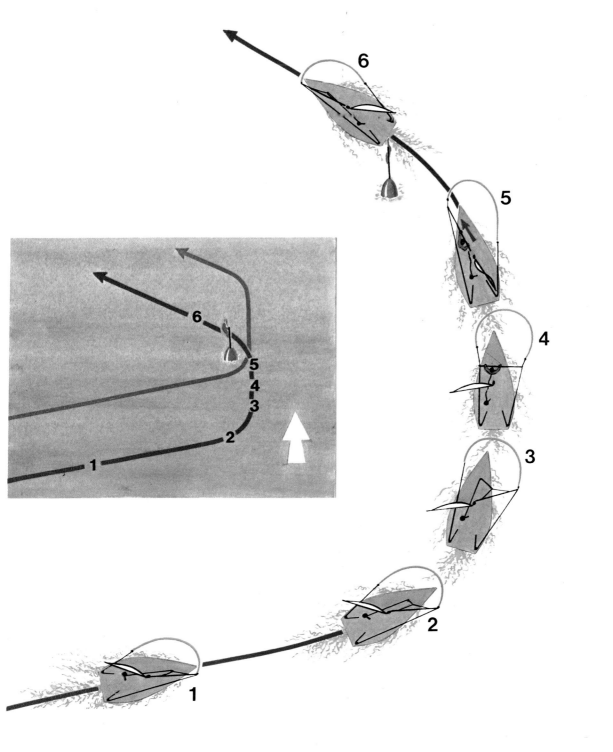

The twin-pole method

A twin-pole gybe from a reach to a reach is really very difficult. If it is to be done properly it means a lot of team work and a lot of preparation to get it right.

The approach to the mark should be even further to windward, thus allowing longer with the wind aft to enable the slower changeover of poles to be accomplished. Before reaching position the second spinnaker pole must be in the mast cup which is then hoisted to the right level. The new guy is brought forward and hooked into the spinnaker pole end.

1 Start to bear away slowly. Lift the new pole until it is the same height as the one in use.

2 Bear away faster, ease out the sheet and square back the pole in use.

3 Hold the boat steady with the wind dead aft. The pole in use is now fully aft. The sheet is eased until it is near the forestay (making sure the snap shackle does not touch it and release itself).

4 Tighten the new guy, thus pulling the new pole two or three feet out to the spinnaker corner. Then gybe the mainsail. At the same time tighten the new sheet and let go the old guy, while the bowman pulls the old pole inboard with the foreguy.

5 Once the guy is free of the old pole the boat can start to luff. Dip the old pole on to the foredeck inside the pulpit and then stow it as soon as is convenient.

6 It is important to fit the jockey pole so that the boat can then be luffed up close to the mark to prevent other boats getting in to take your wind.

Though this is a stable method of gybing, and thus is suited to heavy weather since the sail is always under full control, it is the slowest of all the methods. In particular more time has to be allowed in positions 3 and 4 to set the new pole and dispose of the old. It also needs a large and well-trained crew and the helmsman's role is vital. If in doubt always allow more room on the dead run section.

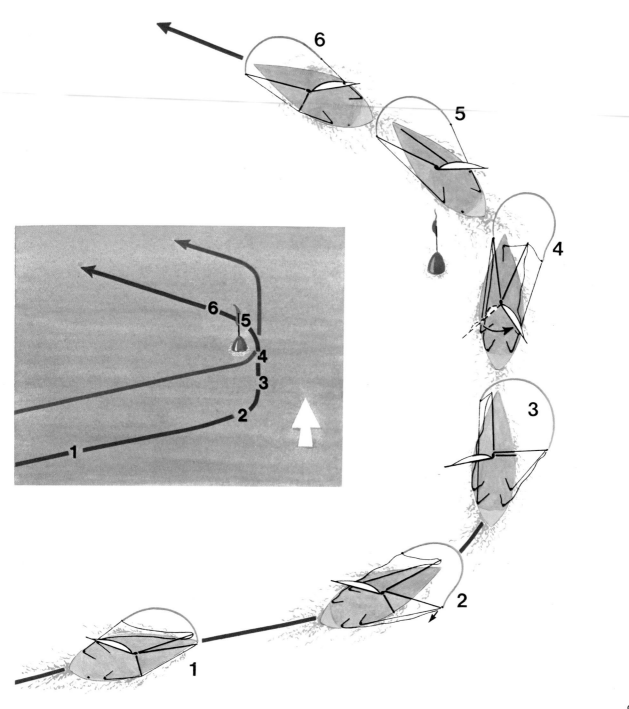

Problems

I must emphasize that success in gybing is largely in the hands of the helmsman who must concentrate absolutely on steering a course consistent with what is going on in the boat. For example, if the helmsman luffs too soon after the gybe, particularly with the end-for-end method, the spinnaker will blow back between the forestay and the mast and it will be impossible for the foredeck hand to set the pole. The only answer will be to bear off on to a dead run again, thus losing a great deal of distance.

With a dip-pole, gybing too soon would cause the spinnaker to collapse to leeward and get out of control. In a hard wind the boat could be laid flat.

Apart from not holding the boat steady, already emphasized, luffing too early is thus the other main cause of gybing problems. In fact, turning the boat at any time during the gybe faster than the crew can do their jobs is a recipe for disaster.

Right: everything went wrong for this boat, struck by a heavy gust just as she was about to gybe. The pole end is already disconnected but the helmsman was unable to keep the boat steady and called the crew aft to try to regain control. The weight of a man on the pulpit of a small boat can make a big difference to balance and so the dipping and reconnecting of the pole end has to be very slick in these conditions.

Below, left: the gybe was, in this case, too slow and the helmsman lost concentration, allowing the spinnaker to collapse. The result is almost inevitably a 'wrap' as it flogs and half fills continually behind the mainsail.

Gybing the big-boy

If you are sure of your crew, and the weather is right – steady wind and not too much sea – why not try gybing the spinnaker and big-boy together?

The only extra gear needed is an additional big-boy sheet, and both must be long enough. Unlike other headsails, the lazy sheet should be passed forward of the big-boy itself before being made fast at the clew, to allow the sail to flap free while gybing.

Assuming a gybe from a run to a run, which is the only practicable case, the sequence goes like this:

1 Prepare to gybe the spinnaker by the dip-pole method. After connecting the new guy you must keep the pole very low.
2 When the helmsman is ready, release the pole from the spinnaker to start the gybe and let go the big-boy sheet so that the sail flies out forward.
3 Gybe the spinnaker and, because the pole has been kept low, the spinnaker will pass between the forestay and the slack luff of the big-boy.

4 Pull the spinnaker through and re-set it on the new gybe. Then tighten and adjust the new big-boy sheet.

Problems

The spinnaker must be low enough and the big-boy luff slack enough to enable the spinnaker to pass across.

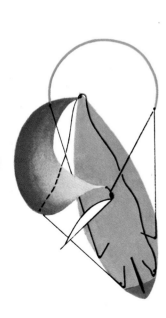

After gybing, the big-boy tack pendant will be wrapped round the forestay. Unclip it and pass it round behind and then reconnect. The halyard also will have a turn around the forestay which can be cleared on lowering. The foredeck crew must remember!

101

Changing spinnakers

The inside peel method

Spinnakers often have to be changed due to course alterations, wind fluctuations or damage. With a good peel change the boat's speed will hardly drop from its maximum.

Assume the boat is reaching. First reeve a second sheet and lead it within reach of the spinnaker trimmer. Also have ready the peeling strop (about 5 feet long with a clip each end; see page 11). Put the packed new spinnaker on the deck or pulpit in its bag or turtle. Clip the new sheet on to the clew. The peeling strop goes on to the tack and then to the stemhead.

The sequence:

1 Hoist the new spinnaker i[n] stops with the sheet slack.
2 Break it out and it will li[ft] against the existing spinnake[r]. Stand by to lower the old spir[n]naker.

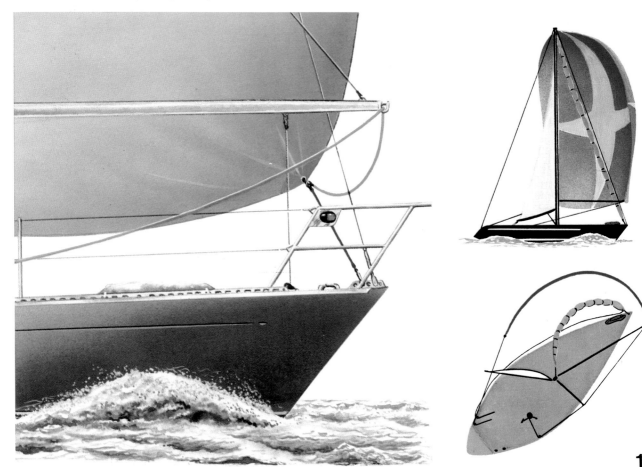

1

3 Trip the tack and pull in the flogging sail with the sheet from the cockpit. The new sail's tack is held by the peeling strop and it can be trimmed via the new sheet. It is not quite so easy to trim, but as soon as possible the guy is eased 6 to 7 feet and connected to the new spinnaker tack. Winch in the guy and, when it has the strain, let go the peeling strop.

4 Set the jockey pole, adjust the guy, trim the sail and the boat is very quickly at full speed again.

Points to note:

The new spinnaker, being different, will almost certainly need the pole height to be adjusted. When close reaching it may be necessary to bear away slightly when peeling to keep the sail full and drawing.

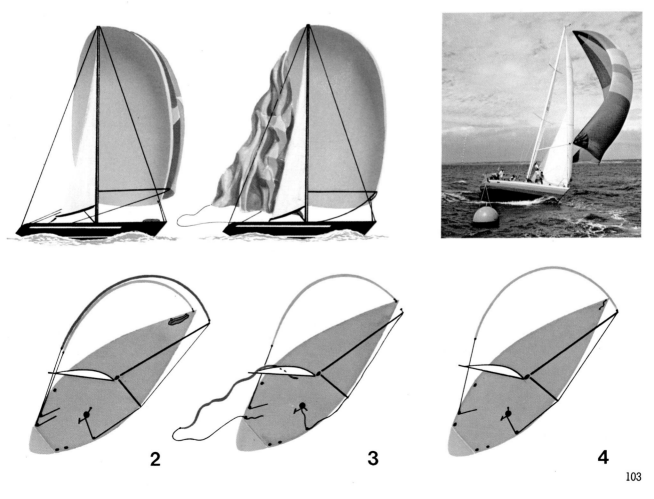

2   **3**   **4**

Other methods of peeling

The method just described was an inside peel, where the new spinnaker went up inside the old spinnaker, and this is the easiest way. In some cases the halyard arrangement does not allow this and then the outside peel method is used. It follows the same sequence but takes a little longer.

Inside peeling with the wind aft is very similar. The sequence is as follows:

1 Hoist the spinnaker, preferably in stops, with the peeling strop and new sheet connected (**A**). Break it out when fully up.

2 When fully broken, trim the sail as best as possible. Ease off the guy also and lower the pole end within reach of the crew (**B**).

3 Release the old spinnaker tack and ease out a few feet of guy. Then clip the guy on to the new spinnaker tack. Release the peeling strop, winch in the guy and re-trim the new sail (**C**). Haul down the old spinnaker.

An outside peel, with the wind aft, is a little more difficult as you have to get the new spinnaker up outside the old one. To do this pull the clew of the old spinnaker in towards the forestay when hoisting the new one (**D**). Once the new sail is up then the old spinnaker sheet can be allowed to go back and rest against it.

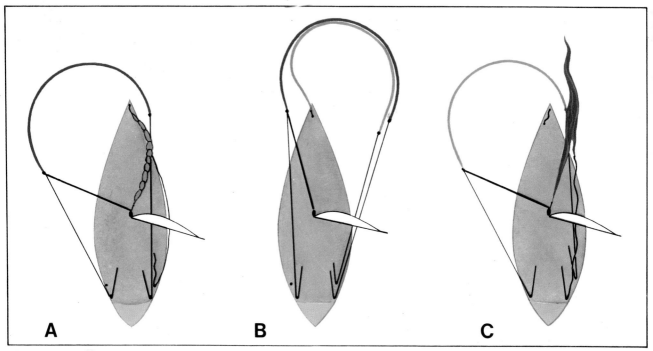

A   **B**   **C**

Points to note:

While all this is going on it is essential that the helmsman keeps the boat at a constant angle to the wind because it is very difficult for the trimmers to adjust the spinnaker sheet or guy when a spinnaker is being changed.

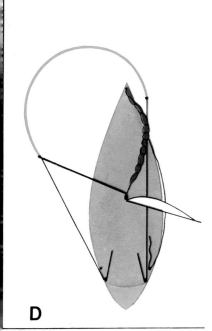

D

Crew duties

For hull trim

The trim of the hull on the water varies according to conditions and is critical for the best speed and control of the boat. The crew must know where to place themselves.

A Reaching in light airs needs bow down trim and a certain amount of leeward heel. So the crew go to leeward by the mast.

B With a light wind from aft the bow down trim must be maintained but the crew should split into two parties as far outboard as possible on each side. In this way they act as wing ballast and reduce the amount of rolling, and thus steady the sails.

C In medium winds, or a bigger sea, the distribution should be the same but move further aft, dead over the pivotal point of the hull. The hull is thus encouraged to find its own trim in amongst the waves.

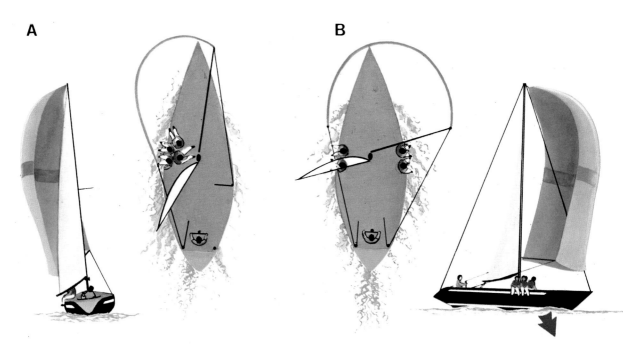

A

B

D When reaching in heavy weather it is essential to get as much righting moment as possible from the crew while keeping the bow up and the stern down, and with the rudder as deep into the water as possible. So everybody who can be spared should be on the windward quarter.

E Running in heavy weather you again have to keep the bow up, the stern down and the rudder as deep in the water as possible. But in this case it is the prevention of rolling which is also needed so the crew should be as far aft as possible and split 50/50 either side of the cockpit.

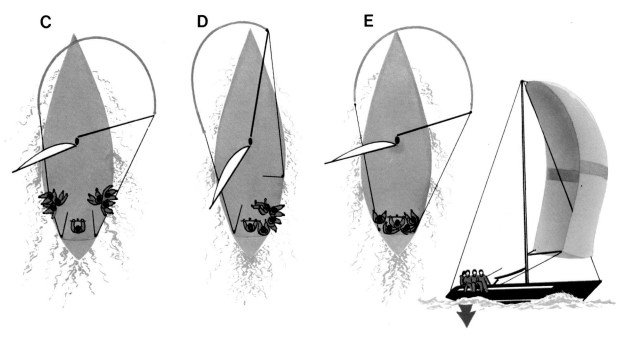

C   **D**   **E**

General sail handling

To run an efficient ship each crew person must know exactly what he or she has to do in any given situation. Before the season's racing starts, have a crew meeting and list each person's responsibilities and their jobs, allocating them according to each individual's size, temperament and ability. For example, the last person you would want on the foredeck is someone weighing 200 lbs with great strength and stamina. He would be more use winding the winches or controlling the mainsheet or even better, what about having him down below! What you need on the foredeck is a lightweight with reflexes like quicksilver and the agility of a monkey.

Once responsibilities are established they should be put to the test by practice. You may find that when you are running through a series of gybes, say, one crew member has more to do than another. In such a case some of his responsibilities can be transferred. Refinements should continue to be made until you have a completely balanced workload.

Example crew duties for a dippole gybe. First draw out a diagram like this, marking in the first positions of the crew. Then go through the sequence, moving the crew about to see if the routine will work.

A   No 1 takes the tack of the big boy to the forehatch and passes it down to No 9. No 2 lowers the big-boy. No 7 (or no 2) lets go the sheet.

B   No 1 picks up the new spinnaker guy and takes it forward. No 5 makes sure it runs free.

C   No 1 calls to no 8 'Ready to gybe!'

D   No 8 steadies the boat and calls 'Gybe ho!' No 7 trips the spinnaker pole end. No 2 lowers the outer end. No 1 pulls on the foreguy to bring the pole forward.

E   No 1 clips on the new guy. No 4 hauls in the mainsheet. No 5 jams off the old spinnaker sheet and stands by with the new guy. No 3 transfers the load from the old guy to the new sheet and passes the sheet end to no 6 who has moved across the boat.

F   No 2 hoists the pole end to its correct height. No 7 gives a hand because of the strain. No 5 tightens and adjusts the new guy; he then releases the old sheet. No 4 lets out the mainsheet. No 8 sets the boat on the new course. No 3 stands by the sheet winch to aid no 6.

G   No 1 moves to the forehatch and clips on the big-boy halyard. No 2 hoists away. No 7 takes the big-boy sheet. No 1 takes the tack forward and clips it on the stemhead.

In a smaller boat some of these duties can be combined. For example, nos 3 and 5, 6 and 7, 7 and 2, or 7 and 9. There are several possible combinations which can be tried. The less running about the better, which is another good reason for the bow man, no 1, to be very light and agile.

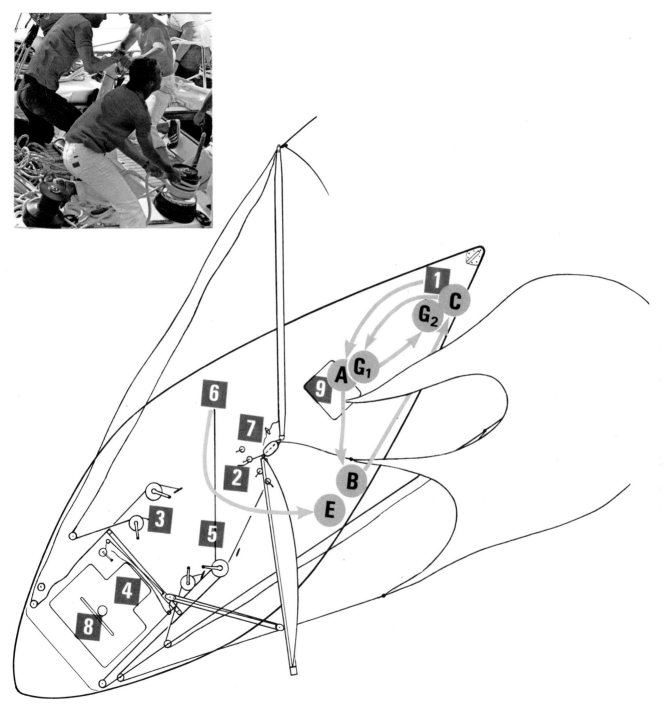

Gybing a small boat

A small boat may only have a crew of three, and so many jobs will have to be duplicated. However, the forces involved are much smaller and so one man can operate all the winches and also the mainsheet for most of the time.

The positions and duties for a gybe might be as follows:

A　Before the gybe no 1 is trimming the spinnaker. No 2 will wind the spinnaker sheet if needed, as well as looking after the guy and the mainsheet.

B　To start the gybe no 2 eases the spinnaker pole lift about a foot and re-cleats it. Then he takes over the sheet and controls both this and the guy. No 1 goes forward to gybe the pole (by the end-for-end method).

C　No 1 gybes the pole. No 3 steers and also controls the mainsheet, gybing it when ready. No 1 clips in the new guy and unclips the old, then goes aft to pick up the new sheet from no 2.

D　No 1 moves forward with the sheet. No 2 tightens the lift and controls the spinnaker pole guy. No 3 steers and adjusts the mainsheet passing it to no 2 when he is ready.

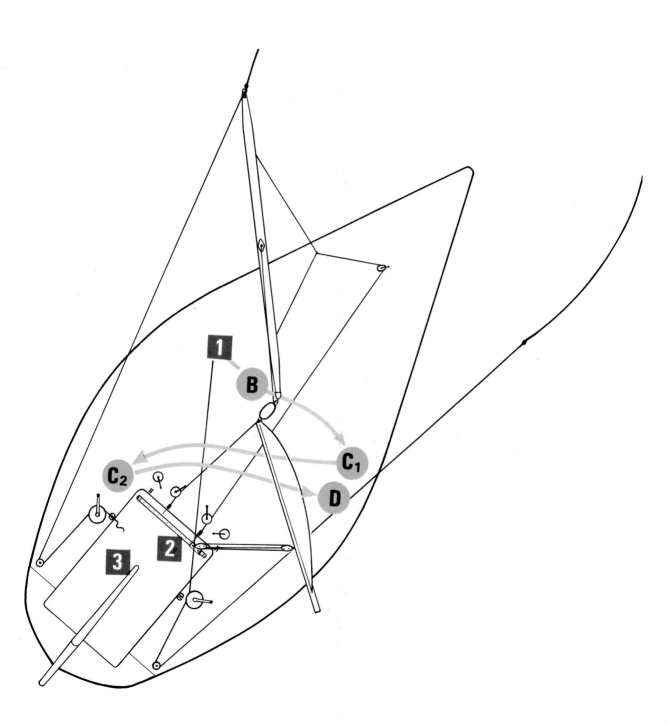

Down wind tactics

Rounding windward marks

The 'golden rule' for rounding any mark when racing is to avoid turning the boat violently. Of course the shortest distance includes the sharpest turn possible, but far more important are a minimum loss of speed on the turn, and allowing the crew enough time to carry out the manoeuvre, both of which call for a smooth, steady turn.

Since other competitors are nearly always involved and threatening interference, the tactics of the rounding must be thought out in advance. This includes when to hoist the spinnaker, whether to sail high or low on the next leg, or whether to gybe if the leg will be a dead run. All of this has a bearing on how the gear and sails are set up, and on which side. Detailed tactics are outside the scope of this book but, in many common situations, I can give some general advice.

First, always try to approach on the tack on which you will continue thereafter. For a port hand mark, approach on starboard tack. This gives time for the pole to be set, the turtle to be in place and the sheets and guys to be connected. Approaching on port tack (**A**) means that very little can be prepared and there are likely to be mistakes in the hurried hoist after the violent turn, besides taking all speed off the boat.

In light winds a smooth wide sweep is even more important to maintain speed and keep the apparent wind well forward for as long as possible (**B**).

After the mark, with other boats close astern, a common mistake is to hoist straight away (**C**). A boat be-

hind only has to remain a little high to travel faster and also to blanket the leader. She then sets her spinnaker without interference and sweeps past (**D**). If leading a group, the counter to this is to sail a little high yourself and not to hoist until the boat behind does so (**E**).

If the next leg is a run, again take a smooth rounding and sail a little to one side of the rhumb line to keep clear air (**F**).

A current will affect tactics in both cases. Allowance must be made for it during the rounding and it will obviously dictate which side of the direct course to sail thereafter. If the current is against the wind it is worth taking a course so that the boat is already turned as it comes abreast of the mark (**G**), and then hoist without delay to get clear.

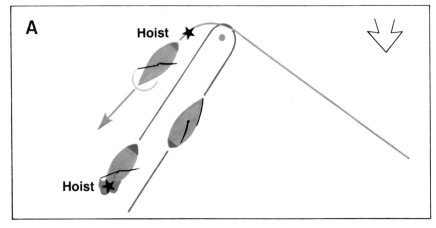

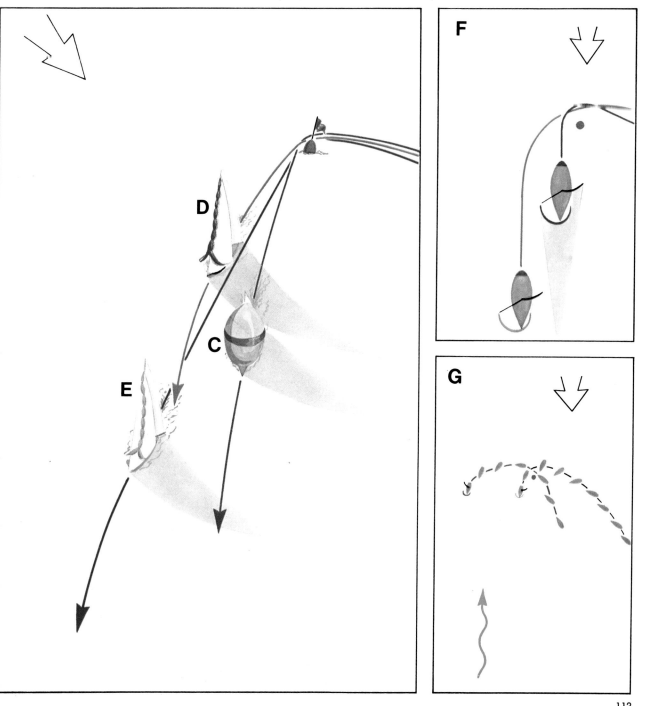

At the gybe mark

The best course for rounding a gybe mark is detailed on pages 92 to 97, but, as usual, the near presence of other boats or of tidal current may force some modification. It is the mark where the greatest distance can be gained or lost too. Always aim to be as close to the mark as possible while gybing. This is difficult since the gybe takes a long time.

The aim should be to finish the reaching leg a little way to windward and then turn on to a dead run for the final approach to the mark. Then gybe a little before the mark and cut in close, luffing hard on the new leg after passing it. This puts you in the best possible position with regard to other boats. The effect of this tactic over a boat going the same speed but taking a more obvious course is indicated in figure **A**. Our boat actually passes astern of the other before the mark but ends up to windward and ahead.

If the current is with the wind this approach is even more favourable but you have to allow plenty for the current both on the initial approach and on the turn. Then aim up high for the whole of the next leg (**B**). Owing to the importance of being to wind-

ward after the gybe it is vital to let the original spinnaker sheet out a long way and to have the pole right forward against the forestay so that the spinnaker can be filled and then trimmed as close as possible.

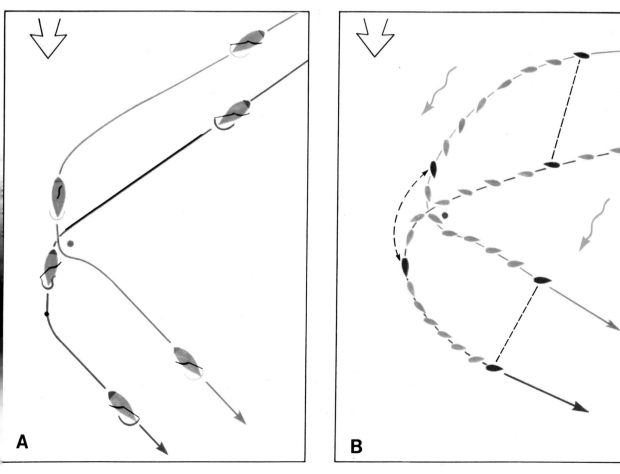

A

B

Around the lee mark

Ideally approach on the same gybe as you will continue afterwards, and from a course somewhat to leeward, if from a reach, or somewhat to the side, if from a run. This will allow a smooth accelerating rounding so that the boat is on course and trimmed as the mark comes abreast (**A**).

Approaching the mark directly will always mean that you end up too far to leeward after the turn and will allow space for other boats to get up to windward afterwards.

As with the gybe mark a windward position is the aim after the mark. If it fails you may be forced to tack clear of another boat's wind shadow, or even to bear away and try to break clear to leeward, losing either speed or weather gauge (**B**). If you can be clear and unobstructed you can then settle down and check compass course, speed, wind angle and get the maximum out of the boat without worry.

An approach against the current needs care since the boat will be swept bodily towards the mark as she turns (**C**). Aim below the mark and only turn when it is almost abreast.

Approaching on a reach with the current, remember to keep well to the windward of the rhumb line and turn early, making sure the spinnaker is stowed in good time. The genoa may already be hoisted but, when approaching on a run, allow time to hoist this sail before lowering the spinnaker (**D**).

On a running leg it is usual to tack down wind, so plan your gybes so that the last one puts you in the best position, far enough away from the mark to make an unhurried spinnaker drop and a smooth rounding (**E**).

If you are forced to approach on the wrong gybe you should luff slightly just before you reach the mark, then bear away on to a dead run and do a gybe-and-drop (or flying drop) as explained on page 80. An experienced crew can save an awkward situation with this tactic which is also useful in match or team racing (**F**).

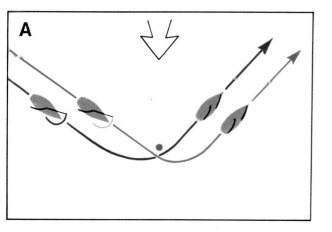

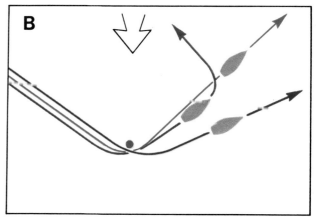

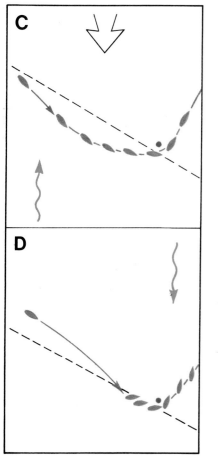

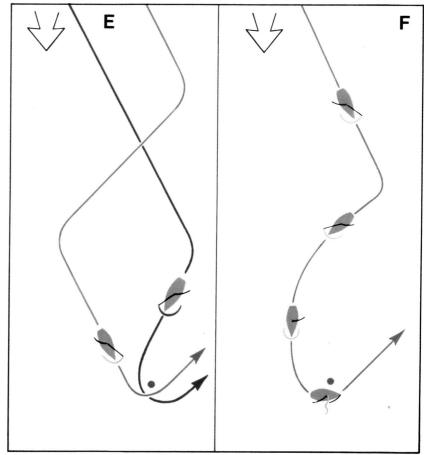

The reaching legs

Tidal influence–the fastest course

On most occasions the fastest way of sailing between two marks is in a straight line. This is of course very easy to do until there is interference from elements such as current. In **A** the green line shows the ideal course. However with the current running at an angle to this it is not possible to point straight down the line to arrive at the mark. You must aim off towards the current. But just how much, because the current over the length of the leg can vary? The best answer is to line up a transit through the mark to some feature on the shore the moment you round the previous mark. Then sail down this transit keeping it steady by aiming off as needed to bring the transit back into coincidence.

If there is no land behind the mark, have someone on the foredeck or, if it is blowing hard, standing just aft of the shroud, with a compass to keep a bearing. The helmsman makes sure that the bearing stays constant the whole way down the leg.

Fleet influence

B shows a typical fleet half-way down the reaching leg. Notice how practically the whole pack has gone to windward of the rhumb line, which is

because the early leaders have been forced up to windward to keep clear of the wind shadows of the boats behind. This is certainly not the fastest route and in the end they will have to come in to the next mark on a very broad reach. The leader is forced to protect himself and this is the only way he can do it.

The red spinnaker boat to leeward in the middle of the pack has been completely blanketed by the wall of sails to windward and will be dropping rapidly back until she can get clear wind. The green spinnaker boat that rounded very nearly last could gain many places owing to this blanketing wall of sails. It is unlikely that she will overtake the boat immediately ahead but should pass the ones to leeward and ahead.

What is interesting is that the blue spinnaker boat which is a long way behind has just gone round the mark and can sail slightly to leeward of the rhumb line without being blanketed. This will be the shortest course and by the time she gets to the next mark those ahead and to windward will be coming down to it on a slow broad reach because they have been forced up to windward earlier. She can come up on a close reach going much faster and by the time she actually rounds the mark she could

have gained on at least half the boats that are ahead.

A spinnaker – or not?

If the first reach is so close that a spinnaker cannot be set while laying the next mark then you have two options. One is as the red track in **C**, ie go as fast as possible on a two-sail reach until you get to a point where you can bear away and set the spinnaker. The other is as the green track where she sets the spinnaker on rounding the mark. She sails as close as she can to the rhumb line with the spinnaker until a point is reached where she can drop it and come up to the mark fast on a two-sail reach.

Which of these two is the best method? I believe that normally the red track is the fastest way because although she did not set her spinnaker initially, she sets it to go down to the mark, and since she will be leaving this mark to port, she will be able to carry the spinnaker right the way round and on to the next reach. The boat on the green track on the other hand has to lower the spinnaker to reach up to the buoy, then gybe and set the spinnaker again. She could lose a lot of valuable time this way.

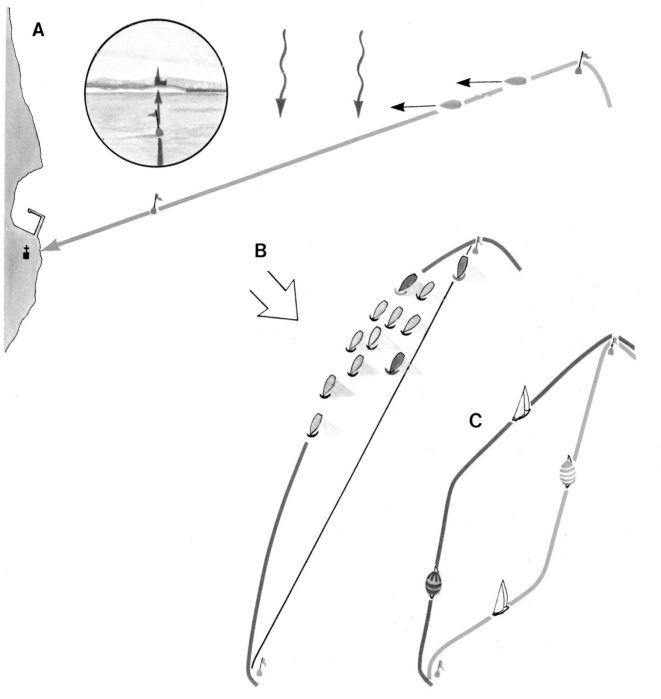

A

B

C

Second reach tactics

A spinnaker – or not?

D shows a rather similar situation to that on the previous page but there is a significant difference in tactics. The wind has gone round sufficiently to make spinnakers impossible when sailing on the rhumb line so we again have two options open to us. One is to round the gybe mark tightly and luff up on to a two-sail reach until high enough to be able to bear away just enough to set the spinnaker. Then we can reach under spinnaker to the leeward mark.

Or we can do as the boat on the green track has done, which is to round the gybe mark with the spinnaker still set and to sail off to leeward until a point is reached where the spinnaker can be lowered and we can point up on to a fast two-sail reach to the leeward mark.

Again, which is the best method? I believe that this time it is the green track which is often the best. This boat has come down to the gybe mark with the spinnaker set, gybed,

and carried on with the spinnaker to leeward of the rhumb line but without losing speed. By lowering the spinnaker later and then coming closer to the wind she is going to be able to reach round the leeward mark and come hard on the wind very quickly without losing any speed.

The boat on the red track has had to lower the spinnaker at the gybe mark, luff up, and set the spinnaker again before coming down to the leeward mark. Then she has to lower it a second time before rounding the mark and luffing up on to her next course. The time taken for these operations is quite considerable and there is always the possibility of a hang-up.

Fleet interference

E is again a situation rather similar to the one on the first reach where it is interference from other boats, rather than the wind angles, which dictate the tactics. A boat on the red track has been forced above the rhumb line because the boats astern are

trying to maintain clear wind by luffing. The boat on the green track has rounded a few boat lengths behind, with nobody interfering, and so is able to go down to leeward without being affected by wind shadow.

As the windward bunch approach the leeward mark they have to bear off on to a dead run with spinnakers set. The leeward boat is able to come up the last little bit close reaching under spinnaker and is going very fast. Because of her high speed on the closer course, and the fact that she does not have to turn through 100°, she can carry her way round this mark without slackening speed. Even though she may just reach the blanketing zone of the red group she will be going so much faster that she may carry her way right through and come round the mark in the lead.

This is a good example of a standard tactic where, if you can keep your wind clear, keep just to leeward of the rhumb line.

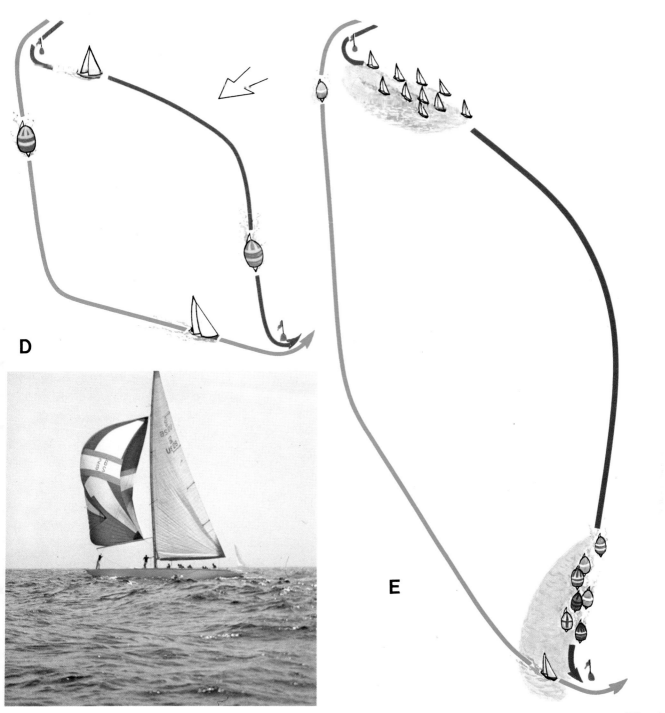

D

E

Tacking down wind

The shortest course
It is standard practice when sailing to windward to keep looking for wind shifts so that you can tack on them. A heading shift, even though of only 5°, means that you can tack on it and so be lifted 5° on the other tack. It is very seldom that you see this happening on a running course though the wind shifts are there just as they are when sailing to windward. **G** shows what I mean.

The boat rounds the mark on the starboard gybe because the wind is slightly on that side of the rhumb line (1). The wind then comes round a little further on a wind shift which enables you to bear away a little more (2). It then swings back so that it is blowing straight down to the leeward mark (3) and the boat would have to be luffed to keep the wind on the quarter to maintain top speed.

The wind then veers so that it is blowing from the other side of the rhumb line (4) and you have the choice of either luffing up still more to keep the wind on the quarter which would take you a long way from the leeward mark, or to gybe and so aim nearer the direct course.

So you gybe to port (5) and the wind then goes round even further and the boat can actually bear away and point to leeward of the next mark (6).

The oscillating pattern of shifts continues so that you can expect the wind to back dead astern again forcing you to luff up, and so on. Although this entails a lot of gybing it certainly keeps the boat on the shortest possible course.

Avoiding wind shadow
While still on the windward leg, study the wind pattern so that when you round the mark the spinnaker boom is set on the correct side.

In **H**1 the wind has backed slightly, so all the boats could set their booms to port and sail directly down the rhumb line without any wind shadow interference. This would be fine providing everybody was prepared to follow the leader, which certainly will not happen. In real life what you find is that boat **a** will luff up so that her wind shadow goes over boat **b**. **b** will do the same to **c** and so on. The only counter is for **b**, **c** and **d** to go up in equal amounts just enough to keep clear of the dreaded wind shadow. But they will find themselves ending up way to windward of the rhumb line and having to gybe to come back down on to it again. The same thing then happens on the other gybe.

A possible answer, if you have confidence in your boat's speed, is that, if **a**, **b** and **c** luff up, then **d** should

bear away so that she falls off leeward of the wind shadow. While the other three are battling it out to windward of her she can then come back on to the normal course and be in the clear (**H**2).

It takes a lot of courage to do this because it will seem that the boats behind come up and go ahead. In actual fact, though they come up they go out to windward, and the only way they can get back down to you again is by going on to a slow dead run or by gybing. If they do that you will gain.

Working out the wind pattern
J shows an example where two boats worked out the wind pattern differently and decided to carry their spinnaker booms on opposite sides. The first bore away and carried on on the starboard gybe. The second boat, just behind, came round, gybed immediately and set the spinnaker pole to port. Note the relative positions of the boats at 1. The boat on the port gybe worked it out correctly and went straight down the rhumb line. At 2 you can see that the first boat has decided that her leg is no good and has had to gybe back (3). By that time it is too late because, as she closes with the second boat, she now has to fall in aft of her wind shadow.

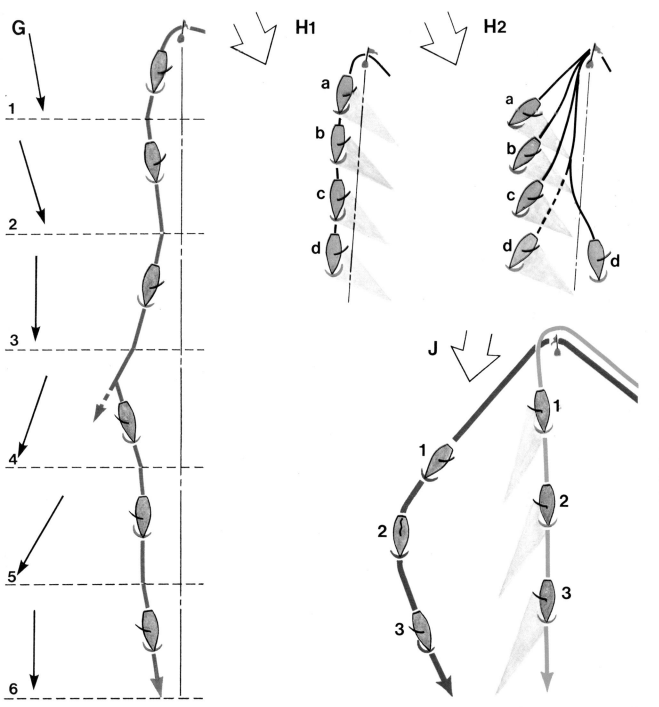

G

H1

H2

J

Covering from ahead

When the wind is dead down the course, so that there is no benefit in using either one gybe or the other, then you should approach the mark on starboard tack. Have the spinnaker ready to set and start off on the run on the starboard gybe. This way you carry your initial speed and momentum for a fair distance. If you were to gybe at the mark you would lose some ground because of having to sail for a short time without a spinnaker, since you would have to gybe before setting it.

In diagram **K**, **b** and **c** have rounded the windward mark and have gone away on the starboard gybe. **a** and **d** have gybed at the mark and then set their spinnakers to go off on the port gybe. **b** will be a little ahead now but will look behind and wonder which of the two gybes is the correct one. Have **a** and **d** seen something that she has not seen? In a situation like this **b**, who has by now gone a fair way to one side of the rhumb line, should gybe on to port to

try to cover both halves of the fleet as an insurance. She really must be very careful and make sure that she does not get in anybody's wind shadow. If she finds that she is being affected, then she must immediately gybe and get away from the disturbed air.

Higher speed – or shorter distance?
The three boats that have rounded the windward mark and are now on the starboard gybe, are running about as dead square as they dare without reaching the angle when boat speed drops off sharply. **a** has decided that if she sails a little closer to the wind then she will go so much faster that she would gain a little distance overall.

At position 2, **a** has gained a considerable amount while **b** and **c** are still running about as square as they can. It looks at the moment as if **a** is a fair distance ahead. However, when they come to position 3 they reach the lay-line for the leeward

mark and they have to gybe. **a**, who has been sailing slightly closer to the wind, has to go a little past the lay-line whereas **b** and **c** have gybed exactly on it and are now running with the wind slightly on the quarter down to the leeward mark.

Notice at this point that **c**, who had been last round the windward mark and had kept her nose tucked to leeward of **b**'s quarter, has now gybed on her windward side and her wind shadow has passed ahead of **b**. So she is technically in the lead.

Position 4 shows three boats, now all converged, at the leeward mark **a**, which has sailed a considerable distance further but faster, has come up to leeward of **b** and **c** but has been unable to get through their wind shadow. **b** cannot get through **c**'s wind shadow and so they have ended up, still in a bunch, at the leeward mark, but with **c** now leading, and **a** now last.

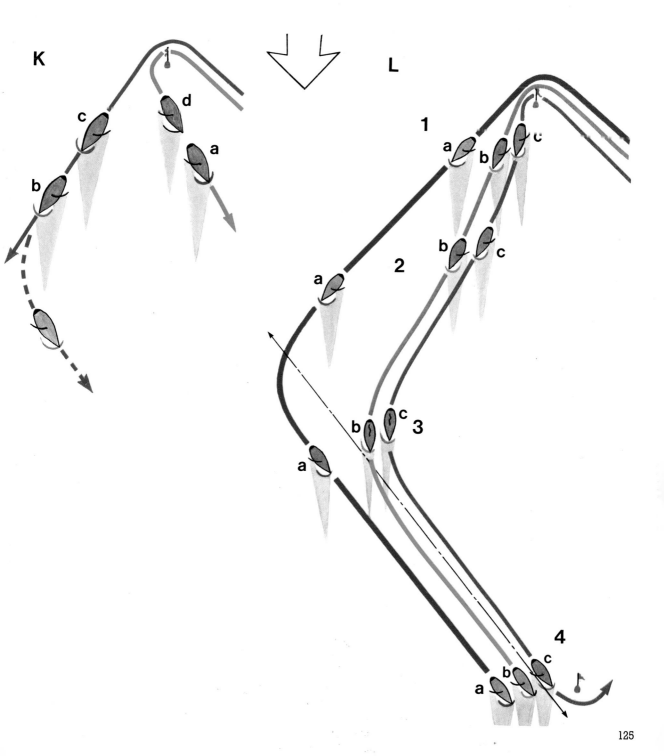

K

L

1

2

3

4

a b c d

Breaking cover

Covering and breaking cover when running need great care in the accuracy of steering and in the timing of manoeuvres. When running down to the leeward mark there is usually a boat dead astern who keeps on trying to take your wind by luffing up. Make sure that you watch and cover her all the time. Stay just ahead of her and slightly to windward of her wind shadow as in position 1. At the same time, keep a good lookout for the leeward mark and check it with a hand-bearing compass so that you know exactly as you are about to approach the layline (ie the angle where you have to gybe, so that when you are pointing at the leeward mark you have the wind at the same angle to your boat, but on the other gybe).

Just before you reach this point you should let the boat behind come up to windward of you as in position 2. At this time she will be so excited at overtaking that she will go a little bit further and faster until she has

gone past you and left you in clear wind again but dead to leeward. If you have timed it correctly you will be at position 3 just approaching the lay-line. It is then that you know you are safe again because from now on, as soon as you gybe, she will immediately gybe also and you will again be ahead of her as in position 4.

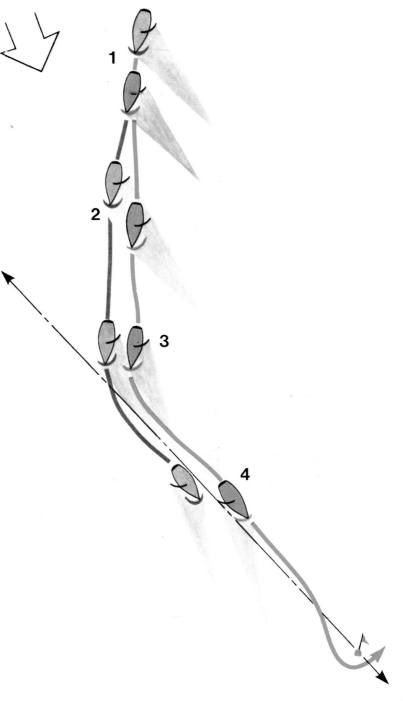

Making a polar diagram

In the chapters on tactics it will have become obvious how important the best sailing angles down wind are ie the sailing angle that gives you maximum speed nearest to the mark. Optimum speed-made-good down wind is very difficult to establish. The problem is that it varies with boat design, height and length of wave, speed of the wind and also the temperature. What we need to know is when to change from one sail to another, when to reef, when to set the spinnaker and which one to go for.

To get to grips with this problem the best way is to make a polar curve diagram for the specific boat. You must keep close records of true wind speeds, true wind angle and water speed with the sails that you have up. If you do a fair bit of sailing, after a little while you will get a series of maximums for various wind angles. If these are then plotted on to a polar graph with a sufficient number of points, it is possible to complete the curve.

Ideally you need graphs for different wind speeds, and perhaps for

rough and smooth water, and even for different temperatures. Quite a formidable undertaking! A nice answer to the display problem is to mark out the graphs on thick card or plywood, cut them out and then mount them superimposed on one another in a stack.

Having completed the graph you will immediately see that the slowest point of sailing off the wind is on a dead run, and that as you bring the wind on the quarter so the boat's speed will increase.

You can easily see also from the diagram the available increase in speed once the boat is far enough off the wind to carry the spinnaker. This point of sudden increase is very important when racing when you have to decide whether or not to set the spinnaker. By bearing off say 5 or 10° you may lose in pointing angle, but the setting of the spinnaker could increase the speed enormously, especially in light weather, and more than make up for the loss. Similarly, the point when the big-boy starts to pay off can be plotted, and the effects of changing headsails or of reefing can be studied.

A word of warning – there is not much point in making a polar diagram unless your instruments are accurate, so make sure these are tested and calibrated before you start.

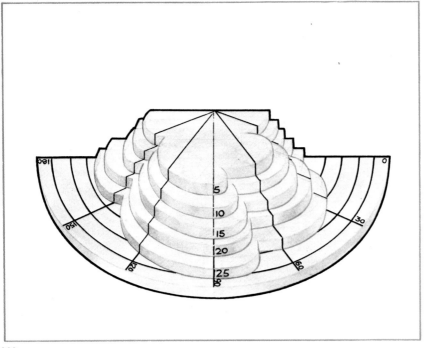

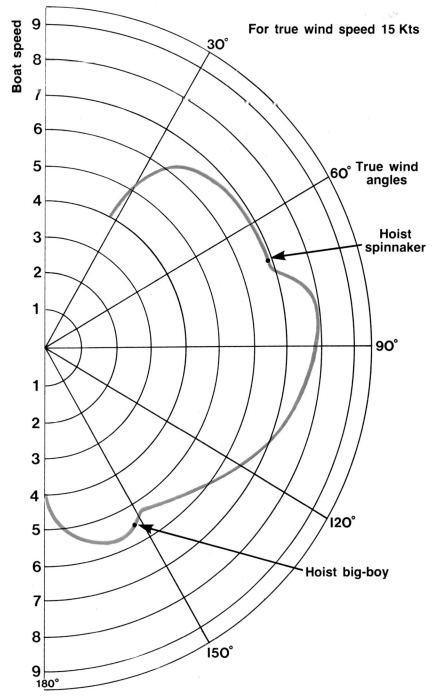

For true wind speed 15 Kts

Boat speed

30°

60° True wind angles

Hoist spinnaker

90°

120°

Hoist big-boy

150°

180°

A sail setting chart

A very useful item to have handy is a sail setting chart for off wind use. The example is for a boat of say 30 to 36 feet overall and, as with a set of polar curves, the best way to make the chart is by trial and error. Spend a few days on open water sailing at different measured angles to the wind with different combinations of sails, and work out exactly which gives you the most boat speed.

Add to your store of information any time that you have a long enough period of steady wind that you have not noted down before. To go to the finest possible detail you must have two charts, one for calm water and one for rough. The one for rough water would be different in so far as all the left hand major stops will move to the right approximately 15 to 20°.

If you do not stock a full suit of sails, then you make up the chart to suit the sails you have on board, and as you add to this wardrobe then experiment with the new sail and insert it on to the chart at a point where it gives the most benefit.

When considering this chart, think also about limitation on the sails you are allowed to carry aboard under the International Offshore

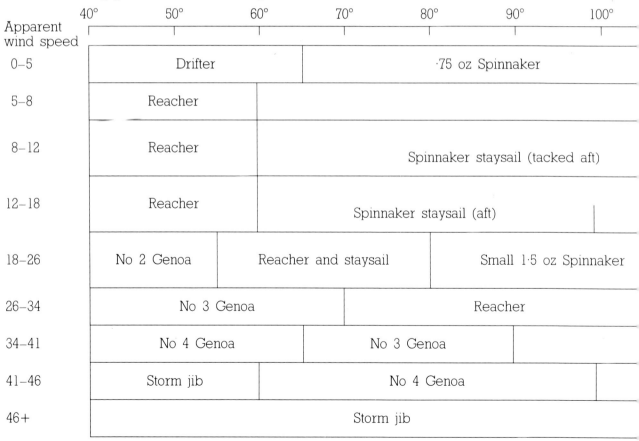

Apparent wind angle

Apparent wind speed	40°	50°	60°	70°	80°	90°	100°
0–5	Drifter			·75 oz Spinnaker			
5–8	Reacher						
8–12	Reacher			Spinnaker staysail (tacked aft)			
12–18	Reacher			Spinnaker staysail (aft)			
18–26	No 2 Genoa		Reacher and staysail		Small 1·5 oz Spinnaker		
26–34	No 3 Genoa			Reacher			
34–41	No 4 Genoa		No 3 Genoa				
41–46	Storm jib		No 4 Genoa				
46+	Storm jib						

Rule. And with this chart at hand you will find it much easier to decide on any certain day which sails should be used just by studying the weather forecast. If the forecast says that the wind will be reasonably light then you can afford to take your 0.5 oz floater on board instead of your 1.5 oz tri-radial. Incidentally, on a long trip, you are likely to meet various weather conditions, and I would strongly recommend that if there is a choice you should always take a 1.5 oz tri-radial spinnaker.

Note that the wind speeds and wind angles given here are all 'apparent'; ie 'over the deck'.

	110°	120°	130°	140°	150°	160°	170°	180°

·5 oz Floater						
·75 oz Spinnaker					·5 oz Floater	
·75 oz Spinnaker						
	Spinnaker staysail (tacked forward)				Big boy	
1 oz Spinnaker						
Spinnaker staysail (forward)					Big boy	
	1 oz Spinnaker					Big boy
	Small 1·5 oz Spinnaker					
Blast reacher			Small 1·5 oz Spinnaker		
	Blast reacher			Winged out headsail		
		No 4 Genoa				

Recording and marking sails

Sails look much the same as each other when in their bags and there can be great confusion amongst the crew when searching for the correct spinnaker unless some foolproof method of marking is used.

First, there should be a complete list of all the sails on board, pinned up where everyone can see it. The list should give the sail type (genoa, big-boy, staysail etc), the weight of cloth, identification marks, fairlead position number and which track should be used, standard apparent wind speed range for this sail, and any other remarks.

There are many ways of marking sails and bags. Usually a colour-coded series of bands is put on the bags. For example, a blue band (**A**) for a headsail, red for a spinnaker, orange for extras such as spinnaker staysails, big-boys (**B**) and so on. The detailed names and weights are also stencilled on the bag and repeated on the sail corner.

A further refinement is to increase the number of colour bands for sails designed for heavier winds ie one blue band for a light genoa; three red bands for a storm spinnaker.

Spinnaker markings must not be forgotten on the bases or ends of turtles or even the head of the sail (**C**). Another point, with spinnakers in particular, is to put arrows on the leech tabling (**D**) pointing towards the head. This will save a great deal of time when only the sail edge can be found on pulling it out of the bag.

COMPLETE SAIL LIST

TYPE	MARKS	SHEETING	WIND SPEED	REMARKS
GENOAS				
GHOSTER	ONE BLUE BAND	INNER TRACK N° 6	0-5 KtS	—
N°1 LIGHT	TWO BLUE BANDS	INNER TRACK N° 10	3-8 KtS	SHEET 6" OFF SPREADERS
N°2 GP	THREE BLUE BANDS	OUTER TRACK N° 4-7	7-14 KtS	—

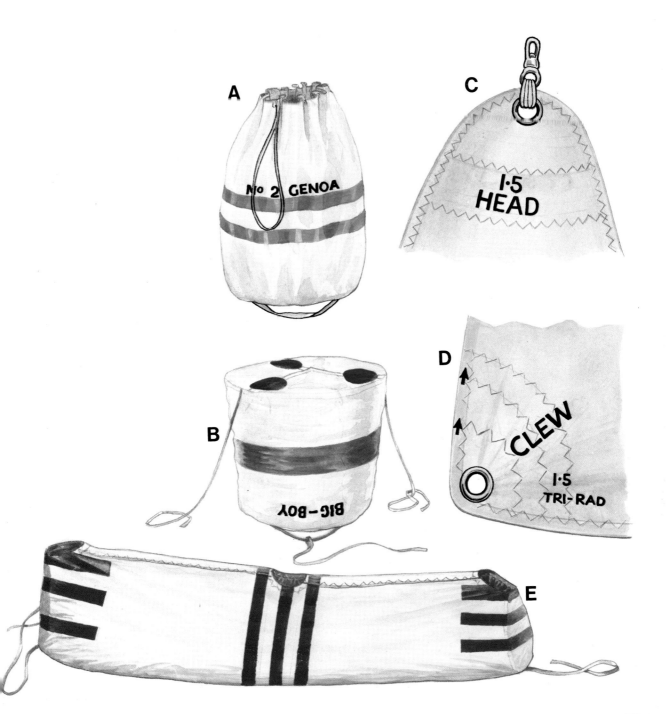

A

No 2 GENOA

C

I·5
HEAD

B

BIG-BOY

D

CLEW

I·5
TRI-RAD

E

Cruising sails

The cruising spinnaker

It is difficult to find different names for the variations of sail which are specifically designed for easy setting down wind with a small and experienced crew. I have given some headings of my own and then tried to explain some of the individual features and subtleties.

The basic type might be called the 'cruising spinnaker' but, as we shall see, this sail does not really have the sort of performance that we are looking for. This is a straightforward spinnaker-like sail, but is asymmetrical with a definite leading luff edge which is longer than the other. The lower forward corner (tack) is tacked down with a strop,

the clew being sheeted in right aft (**A**). Use the sheet like that on a spinnaker, although it is rather a large sail and not particularly manageable or suitable for family cruising. Its advantage is its area – bigger than a genoa and yet smaller than a spinnaker. It does not need a spinnaker boom or guys.

When reaching it can be set as in

A

B. Running, it behaves similarly to the 'cruising chute' and to gybe you would pass the sheet around the forward side of its luff, let it flap out forward and then pull the sail so that the sail flies out to windward on the opposite side of the main boom. In light weather, with a sea running, the rolling could cause the sail to wrap around the forestay, so take care!

B

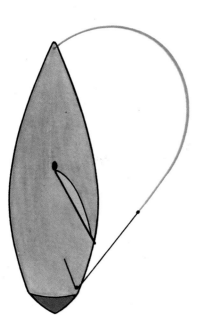

For those who cruise, and like to do so in comfort, there are a number of special cruising sails that are available from many makers. A standard spinnaker is probably the most efficient down wind sail, but it usually needs lots of expensive equipment to control it, and a knowledgeable crew to handle it, both of which are often unavailable to the average cruising person. The new sails are variations on the spinnaker or staysail themes and are designed to set with the minimum of gear and to be handled easily by a small crew.

Using a mizzen

If you have a ketch-rigged cruising boat you can use a mizzen staysail (**C**). This increases the sail area that can be set when reaching off the wind quite substantially. It is easily handled and safe to set, being all inboard. The only problem is that it does not work very well on a dead run, although you can move the tack out on to the windward rail which will help it to clear the mizzen (**D**).

D

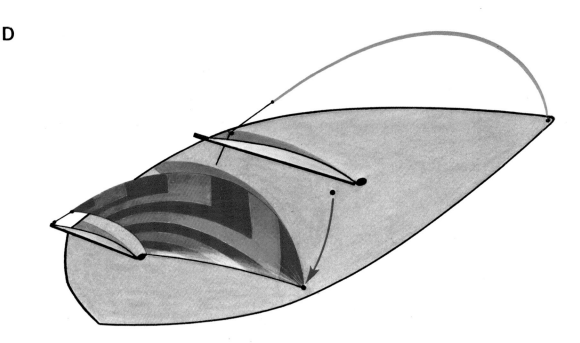

C

The cruising chute

The 'cruising chute' of which there are models supplied by most of the leading sailmakers, was developed from the fan-cut big-boy and has proved ideal for the average cruising boat (**F**).

As with most of these down wind sails for cruisers, the 'chute' is made from 'ripstop' nylon, 1.5 oz for larger boats and 0.75 oz for smaller ones. It is bigger than the standard genoa (**E**) but smaller than the spinnaker. It is usually made with a luff length 2 feet shorter than the forestay, so that it clears the lifelines, and has a high-cut clew to enable it to set well on a dead run.

The sail works well with a wind from forward of the beam right round to dead aft, when you can ease off the halyard and the sheet so that it can be made to fly out to windward.

It then looks like a blooper, but is on the opposite side to the mainsail.

A great advantage is that it has a definite luff so that in a squall, when short-handed, you only have to let go the sheet and allow it to flag. A true spinnaker which has a very much rounded leading edge flogs heavily and often disintegrates in these conditions.

E   **F**

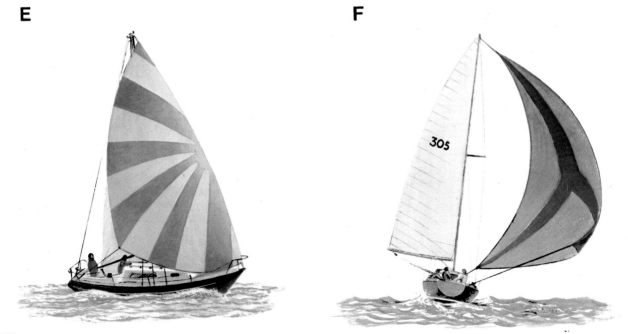

G

H1

H2

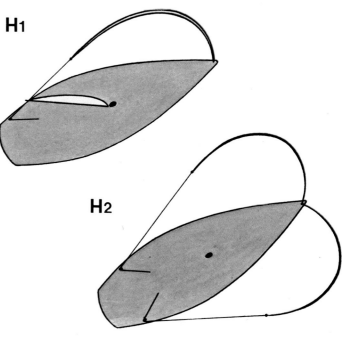

The booster

A variation of the spinnaker chute is very similar, but really consists of two very light sails lying on top of each other. When reaching they lie superimposed as in **H1**. In light airs they can be goose-winged as in **H2** to give a far greater area, still under very easy control.

When doubled the sail has twice the strength and can be used reaching in very hard winds with the mainsail reefed, or lowered altogether. The whole rig can be very stable, manageable and adjustable.